DISCERNING THE SIGNS
OF THE TIMES
SERMONS FOR TODAY AND TOMORROW

CONTENTS

	Preface	ix
I.	Discerning the Signs of the Times	1
II.	Anger and Forgiveness	21
III.	The Age Between the Ages	39
IV.	The Nemesis of Nations	57
V.	The City Which Hath Foundations	73
VI.	Today, Tomorrow and the Eternal	94
VII.	Humour and Faith	111
VIII.	The Power and Weakness of God	132
IX.	Mystery and Meaning	152
X.	The Peace of God	174

PREFACE

THE CHAPTERS of this volume are sermonic essays. They are based upon sermons actually preached in American colleges and universities; but they were not written until after delivery. In the process of putting them in written form they were made somewhat more theological than in their original form. Theoretical points were elaborated in some cases beyond the limits usually deemed advisable in the traditional sermon.

The sermons are divided into two categories. One group deals with the perennial themes of the Christian faith. The other seeks to interpret certain aspects of the Christian faith in terms of their special relevance to the thought and the life of our age. Being a tragic age which has suffered two great world conflicts and which can not yet be certain that it has the moral resources or the political instruments to avoid further world chaos, the primary theme of this category of sermons is the relation of the historical to the trans-historical elements of the Christian faith. The Christian community prays: "Thy kingdom come, thy will be done on earth as it is in heaven" and thereby testifies that it believes in the realization of God's will in human history. But it also confesses with St. Paul: "If in this life only, we had hoped in Christ, we are of all men most miserable," thereby expressing its understanding of the fact that the Christian hope transcends the limits of history as we know it. The sermons are meant to elaborate these two facets of the Christian hope, in the belief that an age confronted with so many possibilities of realizing God's will in new dimensions of historic existence, but also confronting so many historic frustrations, is in particular need of the Christian gospel; and requires both the relative-historical, and the final-and-absolute facets of the Christian hope to maintain its sanity and its sense of the meaning of existence.

REINHOLD NIEBUHR

December, 1945

I

DISCERNING THE SIGNS OF THE TIMES

"The Pharisees also with the Sadducees came, and tempting desired him that he would shew them a sign from heaven. He answered and said unto them, When it is evening, ye say, It will be fair weather: for the sky is red. And in the morning, It will be foul weather today: for the sky is red and lowering. O ye hypocrites, ye can discern the face of the sky; but can ye not discern the signs of the times?" Mt. 16:1-3.

WEATHER forecasting is one of the oldest forms of scientific knowledge. Since the most ancient days fishermen and men of the soil have been wont to look at the sky, to "cock a weather eye" at the rising or setting sun, at the cloud formations and other indices of prospective weather, and make their predictions of sunshine or rain. Every community has had its particularly shrewd forecasters to whom intuitive knowledge was frequently ascribed. But the supposed intuitions were merely unconsciously collated scientific data. They had studied various sequences in the weather, artfully weighed and balanced different variables, and thus arrived at their conclusions. The advance of science has increased the range of weather forecasting; but it is still a good symbol of the reliability of man's objective knowledge when he analyzes the processes of nature. A mistake may be made; but personal interest is not likely to prompt the mistake, or tempt the observer to falsify data, or to draw wrong conclusions from the evidence.

There is thus a reliability in our knowledge of the "face of the sky" which is practically unattainable in our discernment of the "signs of the times." "Signs of the times" include all forms of historical, in contrast to, natural knowledge. To discern the signs of the times means to interpret historical events and values. The interpretation of history includes all judgments we make of the purpose of our own actions and those of others; it includes the assessment of the virtue of our own and other interests, both individual and collective; and finally it includes our interpretation of the meaning of history itself.

The issue which brought the charge of "hypocrisy" from Jesus against those who asked for a "sign from heaven" concerned the ultimate issue about history. The meaning of Messianic expectations was at stake. Messianic expectations were expressions of the idea that history had a certain character and that it moved toward the fulfillment of its purpose. The age of the Messiah was the age in which the obscurities of history would be clarified; its frustrations would be overcome and human life would flower in a community of perfect peace and harmony. There were to be some special "signs" of this approaching end. The Pharisees and Sadducees were asking Jesus to produce these signs in order to validate his Messianic claims.

Jesus' answer implied that the "signs" were already manifest, but that those who desired them could not discern them because of their hypocrisy. The hypocritical element which entered into all Messianic calculations was the egoistic hope that the end of history would give Israel as the chosen nation, or the righteous of Israel, victory over their enemies and final justification in the sight of God and man. This egoistic form of Messianism leads to mistakes and miscalculations not only in regard to the ultimate "end" or meaning of history but in regard to any proximate end. Actually no nation or individual, even the most righteous, is good enough to fulfill God's purposes in history. Jesus' own conception of history was that all men and nations were involved in rebellion against God and that therefore the Messiah would have to be, not so much a strong and good ruler who would help the righteous to be victorious over the unrighteous, but a "suffering servant" who would symbolize and reveal the mercy of God; for only the divine forgiveness could finally overcome the contradictions of history and the enmity between man and God. But no self-righteous man or nation would be able to discern the "signs" (the impending cross, for instance) which would signify this kind of final clarification of history. The lack of discernment would be due, not to a defect of the mind in calculating the course of history, but to a corruption of the heart, which introduced the confusion of selfish pride into the estimate of historical events. This is the basis of our Lord's charge of hypocrisy against those who desired a "sign" of the coming Kingdom. They were morally and spiritually unable to discern the sign of the Kingdom of God, which would not vindicate anyone, not even the righteous man against his foe, but which would rather be a vindication of God against all elements in human history which stood in defiance of His power and goodness.

II

It is not our concern, in this study, to analyze the particular form of hypocrisy which led Jesus' contemporaries to the particular error of misinterpreting the ancient hope of a Messianic reign, but rather to study the difference in the source of error between all forms of historical knowledge and those dealing with the knowledge of nature, i.e., between the "face of the sky" and the "signs of the times." This difference has been obscured in the whole of our modern culture, which fondly assumed that the kind of "objectivity" of which the natural sciences boast may be easily transferred to all historical, political and social judgments. This assumption rests upon a disregard of the partly conscious and partly unconscious dishonesty involved in the error of social and historical judgments. All false judgments of friend or foe, of accepted or rejected social movements, or of any aspect of man's social life and the course of his history, must be charged, at least partly, to hypocrisy. Therefore the elimination of error is never purely an intellectual enterprise but a moral and spiritual one. The highest degree of objectivity and impartiality in the assessment of historical values is achieved by a quality of religious humility, which gains awareness of the unconscious dishonesty of judgment and seeks to correct it.

The difference between the knowledge of nature and the knowledge and estimate of our fellowmen is this: in the knowledge of nature the mind of man is at the center of the process of knowing; and the self with all its fears, hopes and ambitions is on the circumference. In the knowledge of historical events the self, with all its emotions and desires, is at the center of the enterprise; and the mind is on the circumference, serving merely as an instrument of the anxious self. The reason for this difference is obvious. When we look at a flower or a star, at a geological formation or at a problem in chemistry, the prestige and the security of the knower is not involved. The things we see are what they are; and no emotion can change the facts or alter the conclusions. If we try to assess the meaning of some facts of nature for the human enterprise, we are already on a different level of knowledge where the whole weight of human pride and insecurity may be felt. One school of thought may seek to prove that natural history invalidates all human claims to a unique kind of creaturehood among the other creatures; while another school of thought may seek to deny obvious facts of natural history, as for instance the fact of evolution, because these prove man's relation to other creatures and are therefore felt to be an affront to human pride. The whole evolutionary controversy was charged with non-scientific and non-objective factors on both sides. In the one case scientific philosophies were too prone to seek an escape from the unique responsibilities of human freedom; and in the other case orthodox religionists were too anxious to prove too much and to assert the dignity of man by denying his creatureliness.

The conflict over scientific philosophies suggests that any philosophy, even one which claims to rest purely on the science of nature, is on the borderline between the objective knowledge of nature and the subjective and "existential" knowledge of history. Wherever judgments are made about the relation of man to nature, they are a part of a total religious interpretation of life, in which detailed facts of nature and history are brought into a total scheme of meaning. These schemes of meaning are always something more and something less than mere constructs of thought. They are always systems of faith. Such systems must finally deal with man's sense of the meaning of the whole and of his place in that meaning. In seeking to find his own place in the whole, man is always subject to two contradictory temptations. He is tempted on the one hand to claim a too unique and central place in the whole scheme of things; on the other hand he is tempted to flee from his responsibilities by denying the unique place which he has in the created world by virtue of his freedom.

Most philosophies are on the borderline between the knowledge of nature and the knowledge of history. On the borderline there is a mixture of the objective knowledge of nature and the subjectively colored knowledge of human events and purposes. This borderline does not alter the essential contrast between the two types of knowing. When we behold not a flower or a star, but a friend or foe; when we estimate not natural sequences, but the course of human history; when we weigh not the actions and reactions of the atoms of nature, but the ambitions and purposes of our competitors and comrades, we are never disinterested observers. We are always part of the drama of life which we seek to comprehend; and participants in the conflicts and comradeships which we seek to arbitrate or enjoy. Our judgments of others are mixed with emotions prompted by our strength or our weakness in relation to them. Their virtues and advantages may excite our jealousy or prompt our emulation. Their vices may tempt us to hatred. Their weakness may elicit our pity or their strength arouse our fear. We are involved as total personalities in the affairs of history. Our mind is never a pure and abstract intelligence when it functions amidst the complexities of human relations. There is no vantage point, individual or collective, in human history from which we could judge its movements with complete impartiality. There is not even a point in time from which we could judge past events with complete impartiality. It is true of course that some periods of history are, or appear to be, sufficiently dead to seem irrelevant to the contest of interests and values which color our judgments in the present moment. But we can never be sure. Our judgment of Hamilton or Jefferson is still partly determined by contemporary party prejudice; and even an analysis of the causes of the decline of ancient Rome is certain to be mixed with social and political convictions, derived from contemporary situations. That is why the writing of history remains a political weapon. When the Russian communists change their party line, they also give a new and different estimate of the significance of Peter the Great, or even of Ivan the Terrible.

Just as there are only vantage points of relative impartiality in time from which we view the past, so there are only vantage points of relative impartiality from which we view the present scene. All human justice depends upon the organization of relatively impartial judicial instruments, through which the endless conflicts of interest between men are arbitrated. But if the issues reach deep enough into the very foundations of the society upon which the court rests, its judgments become interested judgments. In the international society, no genuine instruments of impartial justice have, as yet, been created. Even a war, which by the common consent of mankind is judged a just war against aggression, prompts some social and political judgments which future generations will regard as partisan prejudices or as expressions of the power, rather than the justice, of the victors.

It is of course important for any society to have as many organs of relative impartiality as possible, both official and unofficial. There is, for instance, a professional group in modern society which is not immediately involved in the contests of power which divide the industrial community. The relative impartiality of such a group may greatly contribute to the mitigation of party animosity. Furthermore, a degree of impartiality may be achieved purely by intellectual process. For the higher and wider the intellectual perspective, the better are men able to see, not merely the interest of their own nation or group, but those of competing groups.

But whatever the merits and achievements of these organs of relative impartiality, there is no place in human history where the affairs of our fellowmen can be viewed in purely intellectual terms. We are always part of the drama of life which we behold; and the emotions of the drama therefore color our beholding.

There is no novelty in this observation. The common sense of mankind has always taken cognizance of these partialities and has shrewdly learned to discount the judgments of interested participants in any enterprise. But little has been done to estimate the moral, as distinguished from the intellectual, factors which are involved in our errors of historical judgment. Marxism, which first developed the theory of the "ideological taint" in our political judgments, regards dishonest rationalizations as primarily due to the finiteness of human perspectives. Engels specifically denies that any element of conscious dishonesty enters into these errors. This is due to the fact that the Marxist theory of human consciousness is too naturalistic to appreciate the indeterminate freedom of man and the consequent transcendence of the self over its limited judgments. Yet Marxist polemics against the "bourgeois" foe always assume the dishonesty which is explicitly disavowed in the Marxist theory of "ideology."

Actually our historical judgments, when carefully

analyzed, reveal a bewildering compound of unconscious ignorance and conscious rationalization of selfish interests. If we think that the second world war was fought for the sake of achieving an "American century," that judgment (which is incidentally remarkably similar to the Messianic errors castigated by Christ) is partly derived from the limited perspective of Americans, who naturally look at the world from an American vantage point. But it is also partly derived from a conscious American pride and will-to-power which would bring the world under American domination.

If a woman underestimates the beauty of a rival that is an error in judgment which can not be corrected by, let us say, a course in æsthetics. Personal jealousies weigh more heavily in such judgments than purely intellectual estimates of beauty. In the treason trial of Marshal Pétain, the Marshal claimed that he was honestly seeking to preserve France in a difficult situation, while his enemies maintained that he used the catastrophe which befell his nation to further personal ambitions, conceived long before. Some witnesses hesitated to charge the defendant with conscious treason; and insisted only that his actions, whatever his motives, were detrimental to the interests of his nation. This restraint was commendable even though the weight of evidence was on the side of those who charged a conscious advancement of personal ambition. The restraint was justified because the mixture of motives in any person is so complex and bewildering that none of us can be certain about any judgments which pretend to search the secret of men's hearts. We can not even be certain about our judgments of our own motives, perhaps least of all about our own. Since we usually do not deceive others without also deceiving ourselves, our motives are frequently "honest" after we have dishonestly constructed the imposing façade of ideal intentions.

The awful evils which arise from race prejudice are regarded by some observers as a form of conscious perversity, and by others as the consequence of mere ignorance. When race prejudice is fully conceived it brings forth the most terrible cruelties. These cruelties would seem to justify the theory of a consciously perverse race pride. Yet the soil out of which they spring is no different in kind than that which nourishes the seemingly harmless false judgments about the virtues and vices of other groups which one meets at practically every dinner conversation. Race pride is actually derived from a mixture of ignorance and anxiety. We judge the other race falsely because we ignorantly make the partial and particular standards of our own group into the final criteria of beauty, virtue or truth. We also judge it falsely because we fear the competitive threat of the other group and seek to discount it.

The combination of ignorance and dishonesty, which determines the composition of our social prejudices, is occasioned by the fact that all men are creatures of limited perspectives and yet are also free spirits who have some knowledge of the larger frame of reference in which their judgment and their interest are not the center of the scheme of things. Our anxieties as weak creatures in competition with other forms of life prompt us to advance our own interests. Our strength as rational and spiritual creatures enables us to advance these interests beyond their rightful range. Our further capacity to recognize the invalidity of these claims means that we must, with some degree of conscious dishonesty, hide our special interests and claims, and merge them with the more universal and general interests.

Thus it is that every party claim and every national judgment, every racial and religious prejudice, and every private estimate of the interests and virtues of other men, is something more and something less than a purely intellectual judgment. From the simplest judgment of our rival and competitor to the most ultimate judgment about the character of human history and the manner of its final fulfillment, we are tempted to error by our anxieties and our pride; and we seek to hide the error by pretension. We can not discern the signs of the times because we are hypocrites.

III

The achievement of a decent measure of honesty in our judgment of our fellowmen, and in our estimate of the meaning of the human drama in which we are involved, is therefore something else than a mere intellectual achievement. It is a religious achievement which requires that the human tendency to claim a final position of judgment, though we are interested participants of the drama, must be overcome. The lurking dishonesty of our judgments by which we hide our own interests in our pretended devotion to the general welfare must be searched out. The implicit indolatry, by which we usurp a more central position in the scheme of things, must be judged. The fact that the real solution of the problem is to triumph over the temptation to idolatry proves that the issue which confronts us has a religious dimension. It can not be solved by ordinary moral idealism; for that always degenerates into self-righteousness. It can be solved only by religious contrition. The prayer of the Psalmist: "Search me, O God, and know my heart: try me, and know my thoughts: And see if there be any wicked way in me, and lead me in the way everlasting" measures the dimension in which our self-judgments must take place. We must recognize that only a divine judgment, more final than our own, can complete the whole structure of meaning in which we are involved; and can discern the hidden dishonesties by which we claim a false finality for our various interested positions in the drama. To ask God to "see if there be any wicked way in me" is to admit the partly conscious and partly unconscious character of the dishonesty of our judgments. If we were not partly conscious of them we would not be prompted to the desire for a searching of the heart from beyond ourself. If we were fully conscious of them we would not require that God "see if there be any wicked way in me." We know and yet we do not know how dishonest we are. In the moment of prayer in which we become more fully conscious of the dishonesty of our judgments, we also achieve a fuller measure of honesty. Out of the humility of prayer grows the charity for comrade and foe. The recognition that we all stand under a more ultimate bar of judgment mitigates the fury of our self-righteousness and partly dissolves the wickedness of our dishonest pretensions.

We do not know the God who judges us except by faith. As Christians we have by faith accepted the revelation of His will and purpose in the love of Christ. We therefore know the criterion of His judgments to be that love. We know that all forms of self-seeking, even the most subtle, fall short of that standard. But we must not claim too much for our knowledge of God and of His judgments. When we do, we merely make God the ally of our interested position in the scheme of things. Christian faith must contritely admit that the Christian, as well as every other religion, has frequently accentuated the fury of party conflict and increased the measure of human pretensions. It has done this to such a degree that secular idealists who strive for intellectual disinterestedness and impartiality have sometimes shamed the community of the faithful and have introduced more charity into the human community than they. These idealists have been prompted to deny the religious solution of this problem because they have so frequently observed religious emotion accentuating, rather than mitigating, the idolatry of man.

The secularists and the faithful alike usually fail to see that religion as such is no cure for human pride and pretension. It is the final battleground between pride and humility. There is no form of the Christian faith, no matter how profound its insights about the finiteness and sinfulness of man and the majesty of God, which can prevent some devotees of that faith from using it to claim God too simply as the ally of this or that human enterprise and as the justification for this or that partial human judgment. But these terrible aberrations of faith also can not invalidate the truth of the final insight of Christian faith in which the God is recognized who stands above (and in some sense against) all human judgments; who judges us even while we judge our foe; who completes the drama of history which we always complete falsely because we make ourselves, our culture, and our nation, the premature center of its completion.

St. Paul perfectly expresses this humility of faith in the words: "With me it is a very small thing that I should be judged of you, or of man's judgment: yea,

I judge not mine own self. For I know nothing by myself; yet am I not hereby justified: but he that judgeth me is the Lord."[1] The sense of a divine judgment beyond all human judgments is rightly apprehended by St. Paul as having a double edge. To find it "a very small thing" to be judged of men means that we recognize the provisional and interested character of judgments which are made against, or for, us by others. We will therefore not be swollen by pride because others think well of us. We will remember that they do not know the secret of our hearts. Perhaps they have been taken in too easily by our dishonest pretensions. Neither will we take their disapproval too seriously. The sense of a more ultimate judgment arms us with the courage to defy the false judgments of the community. The idea that our conscience is purely a social and sociological product is ridiculous in view of the fact that the power of conscience has always been most perfectly expressed when men have defied the mediocre or perverse standards of a given community in the name of a religiously apprehended higher standard. The most fruitful resource for the defiance of tyranny has always been the faith which could declare, "We must obey God rather than man."

But the other edge of the faith which discerns a divine judgment beyond our own is directed against the estimates which we make of ourselves, rather than

[1] I Cor. 4:3-4.

against those made of us by others. "I know nothing by myself," declares St. Paul, "yet am I not hereby justified." We do of course frequently know something against ourselves. We judge the action of yesterday wrong in the contrite contemplation of today. But if that should give us an uneasy conscience we may regain our self-respect by the observation that what we are today must be virtuous; otherwise we could not have found the action of yesterday contrary to virtue. Thus we never know anything against ourselves ultimately. The self is always righteous in its self-analysis and secure in its self-esteem until it feels itself under a more ultimate judgment than its own. Most of us are constitutionally self-righteous as we contend with and against our fellowmen in the great contests of life. We never know anything against ourselves. The only moments in which the self-righteousness is broken are moments of genuine prayer. Yet something of that broken spirit and contrite heart can be carried into the contests of life. If this is done the dishonesties and pretensions which color all our social and historical judgments can be mitigated. We can moderate the hypocrisy which prevents us from discerning the "signs of the times." A measure of charity is insinuated into our judgments of other groups and nations. The condemnation of even a wicked foe is made in "fear and trembling" because we know that even that judgment stands under a more ultimate one. And by that fear and trembling our righteous wrath is saved from degenerating into self-righteous vindictiveness.

This religious humility is also the final source of a truer comprehension of the whole human enterprise. It saves us from expecting a Messiah who will complete history by preferring us to our enemies, or by helping us to achieve an American or Anglo-Saxon century, or possibly a Russian one. The errors and hypocrisies which creep into our various historical judgments always finally culminate in an erroneous conception of the meaning of history and of history's fulfillment. Both the historical conceptions of bourgeois liberalism and of Marxist utopianism are involved in errors, similar to those which Christ castigated in his day. They assumed that history would culminate in either the triumph of the bourgeois classes over their aristocratic foes; or in the triumph of the proletarian classes over their middle-class foes. Actually both the middle classes and the workers have been significant bearers of justice in history. They would have been, and would be, more perfect instruments of justice if they had not been tempted to regard themselves as the final judges and the final redeemers of history. Because of that lack of humility and that new form of pretension, they introduced new forms of injustice into history in the very attempt of abolishing old ones. Other Messianic classes and nations will make the same mistake. That is why the mystery of history can not be resolved except in the divine mercy. And that mercy can only be comprehended and apprehended by those who acknowledge that all classes and groups, all cultures and nations, are tainted with hypocrisy in their judgment of the contestants in and of the whole drama of history.

The wisdom by which we deal with our fellowmen, either as comrades or competitors, is not so much an intellectual achievement as the fruit of a humility which is gained by prayer. The faith through which we understand the meaning of our existence and the fulfillment of that meaning in the divine mercy is, ultimately, a gift of grace and not the consequence of a sophisticated analysis of the signs of the times. We are not merely minds but total personalities. We can deal with immediate issues as minds. But we deal with all ultimate issues as personalities. And we deal with them truly only if not the ignorance of the mind but the pride of the heart has been vanquished.

II

ANGER AND FORGIVENESS

"Be ye angry, and sin not: let not the sun go down upon your wrath: Neither give place to the devil." Eph. 4:26-27.

Anger is the root of both righteousness and sin. We are aroused to anger when men take advantage of us or of those for whom we are concerned; when they violate the dignity of man; or when they commit some other flagrant wrong. We are angry in the presence of injustice because we are emotional as well as rational creatures; and we react in the wholeness of our character to evil. Only a perversely detached person can view the commitment of a wrong without anger; and only a morally callous and indifferent person contemplates evil-doing without emotion.

Yet anger is also the root of much evil. Our emotions are more personal and less detached than our reason. We are inclined to be very unfair when we are angry. If we repay hurt for hurt in anger, we usually repay with very heavy interest. One of the first problems of primitive society was to place some restraints upon vengeance. These restraints gradually grew into the juridical procedure of modern society, in which the community as such assumes responsibility both for restraining the victim and punishing the criminal. It has long been recognized that justice is not served when men are "judges in their own case." The total community has a more detached perspective upon the disputes between citizens and upon the wrong which one may do the other than have the parties to the dispute. Thus we have found a social method of eliminating some of the evil which flows from anger. Yet we continue to face the residual problem of being angry without sinning.

One source of sin in anger lies in the selfish narrowness of our emotions. We are more angry about the hurt done us than that done to others; and we are tempted to repay the hurt twofold, because we overestimate its seriousness. Thus anger brings forth vengeance, which is the egoistic corruption of the sense of justice. All communal schemes of justice have developed through the effort to eliminate the vindictive and egoistic corruption of anger, so that it might bring forth a purer justice.

The second corrupt fruit of anger is hatred. Hatred is the consequence of the persistence of anger. In hatred rational perspectives are falsely mixed with emotion. Emotions are passing; and their fleeting character may sometimes occasion a lack of moral resolution. But on the other hand it is salutary when the emotion of anger is ephemeral. If we begin to brood about the wrong which has been done us, the emotion of anger hardens into hatred of the wrongdoer. That is why St. Paul, in the words of our text, immediately adds to the admonition "Be ye angry, and sin not" the words "Let not the sun go down upon your wrath."

One of the blessings of childhood is the shortness of the child's memory. When their elders do not interfere in the quarrels of their children, the latter usually follow the Scriptural injunction "Let not the sun go down upon your wrath." But the memory of older people, and particularly the collective memory of nations, harbors anger over past wrongs to the point where it poisons all human relations. Consider, for instance, the Irish memory of the wrongs which England once committed as a source of hatred, even after England has done much to atone for past wrongs; or the memories in our own south of Sherman's march to the sea; or the bitter memories of all vanquished people. One of the tragic aspects of human history is the fact that the vanquished have longer memories than the victors. The victors could profitably have longer memories and the vanquished shorter ones.

II

The biblical viewpoint which inspires the admonition, "Be ye angry, and sin not" must be distinguished from all forms of highly rationalized morality which regard the emotions aroused in the struggles of life as in themselves evil. Their approach could be epitomized in the admonition: "Be not angry so that you may not sin." They seek for a position of detachment from the controversies and passions of life. The Stoic attitude toward all passions and emotions is the classic example of this kind of morality. The difficulty with this rationalism is that we are constitutionally creatures of passion and will, as well as of intellect; and we are inevitably and responsibly involved in the disputes and controversies of life as participants. The depreciation of emotion destroys our generous, as well as our hateful, passions. A position of detachment destroys our responsibilities in life's controversies for the sake of avoiding sinful corruptions of those responsibilities. We ought to be angry when wrong is done; but we must learn the difficult art of being angry without sinning.

"When a person does ill by you," declared the Stoic saint, Epictetus, "or speaks ill of you, remember that he acts or speaks from a supposition of doing his duty. . . . Setting out from these principles, you will meekly bear a person who reviles you; for you will say upon every occasion, 'It seemed so to him.' " [1] One need only suggest such advice to, let us say, a Pole in a German concentration camp to realize that there is something wrong with it. It is very good

[1] *The Enchiridion*, XLII.

advice in dealing with all sorts of disputes and conflicts in which both disputants are equally honest and well-intentioned. In such cases it is valuable to try to place oneself in the position of the other in order to mitigate the tendency of regarding any position, in conflict with one's own, as wrong. But when real evil is done such detachment is immoral. The proper attitude toward evil is anger.

The cure of the sin in anger is not an emotional detachment from the issues of life. It is rather an attitude of humility which recognizes the constant temptation to sinful and egoistic corruption in our anger. We can not disavow our responsibilities in the struggles of life; and every effort to find a vantage point of pure objectivity and impartiality in such struggles tends to a disavowal of responsibilities. But we must school ourselves to realize that we are participants, and not detached observers, so that we will not regard our judgment of the foe as a purely disinterested judgment. The root of forgiveness toward the foe lies not in the supposition that he did right in his own sight, as Epictetus suggests; but rather in the recognition of the mutuality of guilt which finally produced the explicit evil against which our anger is aroused.

In the early days of the war with Germany and Japan there were high-minded people who mistook the detachment of Epictetus for the Christian idea of forgiveness. Either they tried to deny that the evil which the Nazis committed was as evil as it seemed; or they insisted that our own position was so tainted with evil that we had no right to resist the evil of tyranny. Such passionless forms of idealism obscure the fact that all decencies in human history have been won by comparatively just men, though themselves tainted with some form of the corruption which aroused their anger, proceeding against flagrant injustice. In times when we seek to evade our responsibilities in the name of a high-minded idealism, it is important to emphasize the righteousness of the anger which injustice arouses, and the rightfulness of harnessing that anger in proceeding against the foe.

But when the foe has been vanquished and the immediate peril of the evil he incarnated has been overcome, it is necessary to emphasize the other aspect of the problem. How little victors seem conscious of the taint of evil in their good, of their share in the evil against which they have fought; of the temptation to pride in their victory and the corruption of vindictiveness in their anger! How quickly they forget the scruples which tempted them to evade their duty in the hour of danger! See how simply the victorious nations speak of the difference between "peace-loving" nations and those who break the peace! Notice how they tend to obscure the fact that the peace of the future depends upon the moderation of the pride of each victor so that they may attain a decent accord with each other. Instead they would make it appear that if only the vanquished foe may remain permanently humbled and maimed, no threat to the world's peace can arise. The tendency to identify our relative justice with ultimate justice, and to regard the foe as congenitally evil, is one of the terrible fruits of the anger which warfare arouses. There is an awful blindness in such anger.

We can trace the baleful consequences of this blindness in personal feuds between individuals. But both the blindness and the consequences are even more marked in the collective life of mankind. There is, for one thing, no relatively impartial court to arbitrate the disputes of nations; and there may not be for a long time to come. Nations are always judges in their own case. The pretension of victors that they are impartial judges is one of the most fruitful sources of vindictiveness. For thus the egoistic corruptions of justice are obscured, except of course to the vanquished. If the vanquished react with cynicism to these pretensions, their natural response is immediately regarded as a further proof of their congenital wickedness.

Any fairly astute observer may discern how the power impulse of this particular victorious nation, and the pride and anxiety of that one, and the special vanity or "point of honor" of another, is the real cause of this particular boundary line or that special measure, ostensibly designed merely to exact just punishment of the vanquished nation and prevent its future aggression. The victors and judges are so obviously interested parties in a great historical dispute; and yet they pretend so transparently to be merely the executors of a divine judgment. The less they believe in a divine judgment which "maketh the judges of the earth as vanity," the more inclined they are to usurp the position of divinity.

Another cause of special temptation to sin in the judgment of nations is the difficulty of dealing with the complexity of guilt and innocency in the nation which has transgressed against the laws of justice. No one can deny that when a nation is corrupted, as for instance Nazi Germany was, the corruption is partly due to the lack of civic virtue of many citizens who are otherwise untainted by the explicit form of the evil which the nation incarnates; and that the consequences of the evil affects even the most healthy parts of the body politic. Yet, on the other hand, there are always elements in even the most evil nation which have withstood that evil more heroically, because they withstood it at closer quarters than the righteous and self-righteous members of the victorious nations. But these complexities, including in addition the endless gradations of guilt and innocency which lie between the overt evil-doers and those who overtly resisted them, are obscured by the blindness of vindictiveness. Even at best, collective guilt can not be punished without involving many innocent. The self-appointed judges of nations ought to have a decent sense of pity for those innocently involved in collective punishment. Instead there is a general disposition to deny the gradations of guilt and to insist upon the total corruption of the enemy, both qualitatively and quantitatively. Such is the blindness of anger when it brings forth the sin of vindictiveness.

There are those who think it is possible to trace a neat dividing line between justice and vengeance; and to avoid the sin of vengeance by these nice distinctions. But rational distinctions alone do not have the power to hold the selfish impulses in check which corrupt justice and transmute it into vengeance. Unless we exact retribution upon the vanquished foe with "fear and trembling," that is, with a consciousness of the precarious and dangerous position of our rôle as judges, and unless we have some sense of a more ultimate and divine judgment, under which both the righteous and the unrighteous are found guilty, our best attempts at justice will still be tainted by vindictiveness. The avoidance of sin in anger is not achieved by a position of detachment but by a recognition of the partisan and partial character of our actions and of the majesty of the divine judgment above all our judgments. Since it is difficult to know whether nations as such ever have any sense of a judgment beyond their own, it is a question whether victorious nations can achieve that degree of humility which would prevent anger from turning into vengeance. It is apparent, at any rate, that some of the endless chain of evil in the history of warfare to the very present moment is due to the fact that collective man does not seem to rise above himself to the point where he senses a judgment beyond himself. Nations are, in other words, constitutionally self-righteous. Yet there is always a possibility that a minority within the nation is able to mediate the divine judgment upon the nation. This was the function of the "saving remnant" in the thought of the prophets. Ideally it is the function of the Church to be the saving remnant of the nation today. But the Church must recognize that there are sensitive secular elements within modern nations, who, though they deny the reality of a divine judgment, are nevertheless frequently more aware of the perils of national pride than many members of the Church. Whatever the source of the moral and religious insight which sets a final bound to the immense self-assurance of nations, particularly of victorious nations, it is important that this insight act as a leaven within national communities. Otherwise the pride and vengeance of nations know no bounds; and vindictive passion dictates terms to the vanquished which approach the morality of the foe and make his repentance impossible.

III

Anger mixed with egotism produces vengeance. Anger mixed with memory and foresight produces hatred. The injunction, "Let not the sun go down upon your wrath," arises from very profound considerations, however impractical and impossible it may be to follow the injunction literally. Confronted with a positive evil we properly react in anger; and there is no possibility of distinguishing fully between the evil and the evil-doer. The advice to hate evil and love the evil-doer is not altogether sound morally; and is also psychologically difficult. It is based upon the supposition that the evil-doer has been prompted merely by ignorance and not by malice. Yet a very great deal of evil is done in malice; and the proper reaction of anger must include the doer as well as the deed.

But the fact that the doer is positively implicated in the evil which he does gives rise to the temptation to identify him too absolutely with the evil. Every war prompts theories of total depravity in the foe. In the past war such theories reached a higher degree of plausibility than ever before, because the malice of the Nazi foe exceeded all previous bounds. Yet these theories are never just. The admonition not to let the sun go down upon our wrath means that the evil deed which has aroused our anger must not be regarded as the complete revelation of the moral resources of the foe. Permanent anger hardens into hatred of the foe; and such hatred assumes that the foe is as evil as his deed.

There are indeed criminals so far past redemption,

at least from the perspective of human society, that we incarcerate them for life or kill them. Some individuals, implicated in collective guilt, as for instance the Nazi leaders in the past war, must be treated as society has always treated its most hopeless criminals. But the guilt of a national society is no more absolute than the guilt of any ordinary transgressor against the laws of society. There is a labyrinth of motives in every heart; and every action, both good and evil, is the consequence of a complicated debate and tension between various tendencies within the soul. Sometimes the most evil deed issues from a character less evil than those who have perpetrated a less overt crime. It is a well-known fact that the murderers' row in a prison frequently contains the best class of the prison's inmates. Their crime was frequently prompted by a momentary passion or fit of desperation, and proceeded from less malice than other ostensibly less serious crimes.

The secret debate of motives in the heart of an individual becomes, in the case of the actions of a nation, a public debate in the moral life of a community. A community must, of course, be corrupt in many ways to desire a tyrannical government such as many of the German people desired; and it must be weak in various ways not to be able to resist the tyrant successfully. Yet the whole tragic decay of a culture and civilization which finally issued in the overt evil of Nazism is not the proof of the total depravity of a people. The hatred which the world has conceived against Germany is natural and inevitable enough. Yet it is not just; and it will sow the seeds of many future evils in our common life. It is important to resist evil in the immediate instance; but it is also wise not to allow the memory of the evil to poison all future relationships. The admonition, "Let not the sun go down upon your wrath," may be too rigorous to be obeyed literally. But the general intention behind the advice is sound. The more the heats and passions of conflict abate, the more terrible becomes the calculated hatred which preserves the viewpoints of the day of battle into the days of peace.

We must finally be reconciled with our foe, lest we both perish in the vicious circle of hatred. To this reconciliation belongs a forgetfulness of the past which gives the foe a chance to prove the better resources of his life.

It will, of course, be argued that such forgetfulness of past crimes is irresponsible. It fails to consider the duty of every society to punish crime and to protect the community from future violations of its laws and securities. It is true that the admonition, taken literally, disavows the foresight and care which the community must exercise. Crimes must be punished both for the sake of convincing the criminal that the immediate advantages of his crime are outweighed by its ultimate consequences; and for the sake of deterring similar acts in the future.

Yet the efficacy of punishment is constantly overestimated. No criminal is ever brought to repentance by punishment alone. In penology, dealing with individuals, society has learned by painful experience that severity of punishment guarantees neither repentance of the criminal nor the deterrence of others who might be tempted to a similar crime. Therefore, thoughtful forms of penology, designed to reconstruct the criminal by discovering the residual moral health in his character, have gradually replaced the more ruthless forms of punishment. All of these are in a sense applications of the injunction, "Let not the sun go down upon your wrath," for the realization of the limited efficacy of punishment implies a recognition of the short-range power of anger. Anger against evil is the necessary immediate reaction; but long-range considerations require that anger be abated in order that we may, in soberness of spirit, seek the best means of restoring the evil-doer to moral health.

The injunction, "Let not the sun go down upon your wrath," achieves a special relevance in a war in which the immediate consequences of our wrath against immediate wrong have contrived a more terrible punishment than we could have consciously devised. The cities of Japan and Germany lie in ruins. Highly industrialized communities have been reduced to the simplicities and privations of primitive society. Mighty cities are mere heaps of rubble. If the wickedness of modern aggressor nations has been more terrible than previous violations of justice, so also is the punishment more terrible which total defeat in a total war entails.

This punishment may not incline the heart of the foe to repentance; but if it does not, no calculated increase of the punishment will. The conferences of the victorious great powers, solemnly deciding to hold the victors completely in the chains of an indefinite occupation, and seeking by mere punishment both to turn the heart of the foe to repentance and to maim his power sufficiently to make him incapable of future wrong-doing, present us with the most pathetic symbols of the vainglory of man. How easily we assume the position of the Almighty, in both our sense of power and our sense of justice. How little we realize that the two objects of punishment—to maim the power of the foe and to turn his heart to repentance—are incompatible. If we accomplish the one, we can not achieve the other. How completely we fail to recognize that the sword of the victor is a very confusing symbol of the divine justice under which alone repentance is possible! Our cause was just enough in the immediate instance. But our effort to draw upon the prestige of that justice for untold years transmutes justice into injustice. If only we could understand the wisdom of not letting the sun go down upon our wrath.

Efforts to prolong judgment and punishment indefinitely spring from a failure to recognize our limitations as creatures and as interested participants in the struggles of life. They are informed by man's most fruitful source of sin: his pretensions to a power and a goodness which men do not possess. Thus the effort to maim a foe, so that he will not hurt us again, may incite him to a fury of resentment upon which we did not calculate; and in his fury he may be prompted to the ingenuity of inventing other weapons for those we have taken from him. And the effort to become the permanent judges of the vanquished becomes increasingly subject to the challenge of cynicism. If the community of nations had genuine instruments of juridical impartiality, these evils could be mitigated. But the international instruments we have do not approach the impartiality of the courts of our long-established national communities. They are, and will remain for a long time, the instruments of the power of victors. They do not have the resources to mitigate the pride of victors in the name and the power of a higher justice.

One of the profoundest insights of the Hebraic prophets was their conception of the various nations of the world acting as the executors of divine judgment. Yet each of the nations was itself finally brought under the same divine judgment of which it had been the executor. The reason for this change was always the same. The nations assumed that their special mission under divine providence gave them some special security, or proved that they possessed some special virtue. They were, in short, tempted to pretension by the very success of their mission; and thus came in turn under divine judgment.

They failed to recognize the limited character of all human missions and the short run of all "manifest destinies." This prophetic interpretation of historical events springs from the same wisdom which prompts the injunction, "Let not the sun go down upon your wrath." The wrath of the righteous man against injustice is an engine of virtue in a given moment. But if it is unduly prolonged and proudly seeks to clothe itself in the garments of divine justice, its very pretensions become the source of a new injustice. Man is a creature of the day and hour. Since he also has the capacity to transcend days and hours and look into the past for lessons and into the future for promises and perils, it is neither possible nor right to limit him to the day and hour. Yet the biblical injunction, "Let not the sun go down upon your wrath," just as the warning, "Take therefore no thought for the morrow," are essentially right, though not literally observable. They are warnings to men not to forget the limited character of their insight into the future, and the partial character of their justice, and the short-range virtue of their anger.

We are called upon again and again to be executors of divine judgment. But in the ultimate sense another word of St. Paul, springing from the same wisdom of faith which prompted the words of our text, is true:

"Dearly beloved, avenge not yourselves, but rather give place unto wrath: for it is written, Vengeance is mine; I will repay, saith the Lord."[1]

These words are not only ultimately true but especially relevant at the end of a great conflict in which the vengeance of God upon evil-doers has been more terrible than any which human calculation could have devised.

[1] Rom. 12:19.

III

THE AGE BETWEEN THE AGES

> "*Thus saith Hezekiah, This day is a day of trouble, and of rebuke, and blasphemy: for the children are come to the birth, and there is not strength to bring forth.*" II Kings 19:3.

THESE pessimistic words were spoken by Hezekiah, King of Judah, when he faced a crisis in Judah's relation with Assyria and was threatened with defeat and enslavement by the great power. The words are as applicable to our own day as to his. We are living in an age between the ages in which children are coming to birth, but there is not strength to bring forth. We can see clearly what ought to be done to bring order and peace into the lives of the nations; but we do not have the strength to do what we ought. A few hardy optimists imagine that the end of the second world war represents the end of our troubles; and that the world is now firmly set upon the path of peace. Yet it does not require a very profound survey of the available historical resources to realize that our day of trouble is not over; that in fact this generation of mankind is destined to live in a tragic era between two ages. It is an era when "one age is dead and the other is powerless to be born." The age of absolute national sovereignty is over; but the age of international order under political instruments, powerful enough to regulate the relations of nations and to compose their competing desires, is not yet born. The age of "free enterprise," when the new vitalities of a technical civilization were expected to regulate themselves, is also over. But the age in which justice is to be achieved, and yet freedom maintained, by a wise regulation of the complex economic interdependence of modern man, is powerless to be born.

I

The lack of "strength to bring forth" a newly conceived life, ordained to birth, is a significant weakness of human life not shared by the animals. In animal existence there are always instinctive and vital resources sufficient for every necessary process, including the generative one. Animals bring forth easily, giving birth with little pain, as they die without fear. Human beings are born in pain; and frequently the strength to bring forth must be augmented by all kinds of obstetrical aid. The special difficulties of human birth were matters of observation at a very early date in human history and in the story of the Fall in the book of Genesis the pains of childbirth are interpreted as God's curse upon the sinful Eve: "In sorrow shalt thou bring forth children." There is a profound truth in this myth even though we would not now regard the pains of birth as an explicit punishment of sin. The truth in the myth is that human life distinguishes itself from animal existence by its greater freedom and the consequent possibility of the misuse of freedom. Though the biological processes in man are prompted by instinct, as in animal life, only a few of them are purely instinctive. Generally an area of freedom is left open, where the human will is fused with the instincts of nature. Thus man's sexual life is not limited to the procreative process, but can, by imagination and will, become the source of a wider spiritual and artistic creativity, and also of a destructive perversity.

In the same way the process of birth is not completed by purely instinctive power. It is more painful than animal birth, partly because of physiological reasons, which are, however, related to man's uniqueness in the animal world—the size of the human infant's head, for instance. Being more painful, it can be evaded and avoided, for human freedom has now contrived methods of arresting the natural process of procreation. If it is not avoided, the human will, as well as obstetrical devices, must aid and abet the instinctive forces of nature to create the strength to bring forth. A noted gynecologist once observed that the power to bring forth in the human mother contained a bewildering mixture of spiritual and natural elements. Among the spiritual elements, the fear of death in the mother was marvellously compounded with the desire to bring forth life.

Yet physical birth in human beings is sufficiently close to nature to proceed, on the whole, by nature's laws and forces. It is when men deal with the organisms of their social existence, with their political and economic and cultural institutions, that the pains of birth and the lack of strength to bring forth becomes more fully apparent. All social institutions are partly subject to nature. In the early stages of human existence, at least, they are born, they grow, and die with only slight interventions of the human will. But as these institutions become more and more the creations of the mind and will, their birth and death are increasingly subject to the defects of the will. Modern social institutions are the artifact of the warrior's prowess, the statesman's skill and the community's imagination. With this development the hiatus between the social task, made urgent by historic development, and the moral power required to do what ought to be done, continually widens.

The fact that world-wide economic and technical interdependence between the nations makes a world-wide system of justice necessary is so obvious that even the most casual observers have become convinced of it. At the beginning of this century, before two world wars had chastened the mood of our culture, it was assumed that the comprehension of an historic task would guarantee its achievement. Since then we have learned that a potential world community may announce itself in history through world conflicts; and that some of the very instruments which were to guarantee the achievement of world-wide community could be used to sharpen conflict and give it global dimensions.

But even now we are not ready to measure the full depth of the problem of man's lack of strength to bring forth the historical new-birth required in a new age. The lack of strength to bring forth is usually interpreted as the consequence of a natural or cultural "lag." The common theory is that the mind is more daring and free in its comprehension of historical tasks than are the emotional and volitional forces which furnish the strength to do. Natural passions and cultural institutions supposedly offer a force of inertia against the more inclusive tasks which the mind envisages.

This idea of a cultural lag is plausible enough, and partly true. But it does not represent the whole truth about the defect of our will. It obscures the positive and spiritual element in our resistance to necessary change. The lower and narrower loyalties which stand against the newer and wider loyalties are armed not merely with the force of natural inertia, but with the guile of spirit and the stubbornness of all forms of idolatry in human history.

II

Consider, for instance, the position of the great powers in the present world arrangements. Three great powers have achieved a dominant position in the world; and the charter of the new world organization gives them an explicit hegemony in world affairs. The new world charter speaks loftily of this arrangement as one in which the nations of the world "confer upon the Security Council [which is the organ of the great nations] primary responsibility for the maintenance of international peace and security." Everyone knows that the smaller nations have not willingly conferred such broad powers upon the great nations. The great nations have assumed their rights and powers. They alone wrote the first draft of the present world charter, which the smaller nations tried vainly to amend in principle—though they succeeded in circumscribing the authority of the great powers in some details.

It is also obvious that the great nations are not absolutely single-minded in their desire to maintain the peace of the world. They undoubtedly desire to do so; but each also desires to preserve or enhance its own power and influence. This is the law in their members which wars against the law that is in their minds. The great nations are "of two minds." This is a collective and vivid expression of a general human situation. The "law in our members" is never merely the inertia of "nature" against the more inclusive duties which the mind envisages. It is a spiritual force, compounded of strength and weakness. It is the pride of the powerful, not wishing to share their power. It is also the anxiety of weakness; for even powerful nations are not as secure as they pretend to be. In their anxiety they seek to make themselves independently secure even against their partners in a common world undertaking; and their very effort to do so partly destroys the common security which they pretend to (and in a measure actually do) seek.

All birth in the realm of man's historic institutions is rebirth. The old self must die in order that the new self may be born. The new self is a truer self, precisely because it is more intimately and organically bound to, and involved in, the life of its partners in the human enterprise. But the new self, whether in men or in nations, can not be born if the old self evades the death of repentance, seeking rather to reestablish itself in its old security and old isolation. The tragic events of recent history have proved that old security to be insecure; and the old isolation to be death. There is, therefore, a genuine desire for a new birth and a wider and more mutual security. But it is not powerful enough to destroy the other and older desires. Thus we see the old human drama on a collective and a world scale. If "the strength to bring forth" is lacking in a new period of history, the lack is therefore something else than a natural or a cultural "lag." There is a positive spiritual force in the power which weakens the will to bring forth.

Whatever our hopes for world peace, we must realize that our prospective security against international anarchy is not as good as that of the Pax Romana. This is not because we are worse than the Romans were, but simply because there are three sources of power, rather than one, in the scheme of order. There are too many possibilities of friction between the three, and too many justified mutual apprehensions, to permit the hope that their combined power will give the world an island of order from which to operate against the sea of international anarchy.

Even if the great powers, which have primary responsibility for world order, were more perfectly agreed than they are, we would still face the problem of transmuting the order, which their authority achieves, into genuine justice. The first task of government is to create order by preponderant power. The second task is to create justice. Justice requires that there be some inner and moral checks upon the wielders of power; and that the community also place some social checks upon them. Neither the inner moral checks, nor the outer social and political checks, are sufficient by themselves. Men are never good enough to wield power over their fellowmen, whatever inner checks of conscience may operate in them, without also being subject to outer and social checks.

The great powers in the present world situation

have seen to it that these social and political checks are minimal. Neither the smaller powers nor the subject peoples have been given constitutional instruments adequate for the achievement of genuine justice. The great powers pretend that these checks are not necessary because they, the great powers, are "peace-loving" and just. This is somewhat analogous to the pretensions of absolute monarchs of another age who claimed that they were responsible only to God, and not to their fellowmen. Then, as now, it was argued that a wider sharing of responsibility would encourage anarchy. In both cases there was an element of truth in the contention. There is indeed a period in the growth of both national and international communities in which the constitutional instruments, and the organic sources of social harmony, are not adequate for the achievement of harmony, except upon an absolutistic basis. But in both cases the wielders of power tend to obscure the egoistic corruptions of their sense of responsibility. Ages of international constitutional struggles must intervene before the centers of power in the international community are brought under the same adequate checks which now exist in democratic communities. This struggle will be a long and tortuous one, partly because the self-righteousness of the great powers will resist the efforts at greater justice. This self-righteousness is no natural force of inertia. It is a spiritual force. Self-righteousness is one of the oldest and most persistent forms of human sin. In it the human spirit seeks to obscure the partly conscious sense of being involved in universal human sin; just as the lust for power seeks to overcome the partly acknowledged social and historic insecurity.

Our recent experience with a very explicit and demonic form of national egotism and imperialism, in the Nazi state, tends to aggravate these various forms of national self-righteousness. For the nations which now bear responsibility for world peace and justice are obviously more just than were the Nazis. They are tempted to regard that moral superiority as adequate for the achievement of justice. Yet there have been many wielders of power, in both the national and international community, who have been better than the Nazi tyrants and yet have not been just enough to grant real justice to the weak. The destruction of the most tyrannical centers of power in the community, national or international, does not guarantee justice. It merely creates the minimal conditions under which the struggle for justice may take place with some hope of success.

The will-to-power of the great nations, which involves them in vicious circles of mutual fears, is a manifestation of an age-old force in human history. It accentuates the insecurity which it is intended to destroy. It is never completely overcome in man's history; but every new communal advance requires that it be overcome upon a new level of man's common enterprise. Mutual fears lead so inevitably into overt conflict that one would suppose that the nations would recognize this danger more clearly, and would take more explicit steps for a complete international partnership. The fact that they do not can not be attributed merely to ignorance or the cultural lag. There is an element of perversity in this failure to see the obvious; and in the unwillingness to act upon the facts and implications which are seen. The stupidity of sin is in this darkness. "They became vain in their imaginations, and their foolish heart was darkened," is the way St. Paul describes this fact in human life. That description fits the international situation exactly.

The self-righteousness of the great powers, in their pretension that they are safe custodians and protectors of the rights of small nations and dependent peoples, is also a "vain imagination." Just as the will-to-power is intended to overcome the natural insecurity of men and nations, but actually increases what it would overcome; so also the moral pride of peoples seeks to obscure their common involvement in the sins of nations, but actually accentuates what it intends to hide. Both of these forms of vain imagination contribute to the spiritual impotence which prevents the necessary next step in the development of the human community.

There are, of course, special and peculiar forms of these sins, and special and unique reasons for them, in the case of particular nations, which exhibit the general tendency in variable terms. Thus Russia may have a special form of insecurity, derived from the dogma in its religion of an inexorable conflict between capitalist and communist nations. And its special form of pride may be rooted in the idea that it is the only nation which stands on the other side of a revolution, which, according to its faith, proves that it is purged of the common sins of other peoples. The simplicity with which Russia brands any opponents of its policies as fascists reveals this special form of spiritual pride. Britain may possess a special form of insecurity because she is not quite as strong as the two other partners in the hegemony of nations; and she may possess a special form of pride derived from the superior political astuteness achieved through longer experience in world relations. The phenomenal economic power of the American nation is the source of a special temptation to pride; and the political immaturity of the nation tempts it to a peculiar form of insecurity as it moves into the uncharted waters of world politics. Each one of these special sources of either insecurity or compensating pride is a special hazard to the creation of a world community. Yet they all are merely unique manifestations of the general character of the defect of the human will.

The great powers offer vivid examples of the spiritual impotence of our day. But equally valid illustrations could be drawn from the life of the less potent nations. The smaller as well as the larger nations cling desperately to a form of national sovereignty which is incompatible with the requirements of a new age. Each of them, moreover, has its own characteristic weaknesses. The hurt pride of France and her difficulty in acknowledging to herself that her internal decay contributed to the ignominy of her defeat makes her particularly truculent in her relations with other peoples. Resentment and fear determine her relations to a vanquished, but still potentially more powerful, foe; and the dream of reestablishing her military might seems more important to her than becoming the creative center of a continental reconstruction.

China, whose manifest destiny is to become the center of order in Asia, shows little capacity for fulfilling her appointed task. Lacking sufficient resources for her own unity, she may well be divided by the greater powers into their own spheres of influence. Her impotence will tempt the great powers to venture further into Asia than they ought. The peace of the world is not served by the dominance of western powers in the affairs of Asia. Wherever we turn we find not only general, but specific, forms of spiritual and political impotence. The nations are not prepared to create the kind of moral and political order which a technical civilization requires.

III

The failure of this age to achieve adequate instruments of international order is matched by, and related to, the concomitant failure to solve the problem of economic justice within each nation. Modern technics have centralized economic power and aggravated the problem of achieving justice between the various groups of a national community. While a liberal culture sought for an easy solution of the problem of justice, the growing disproportions of economic power transmuted the static injustices of a feudal-agrarian order into the dynamic injustices of technical civilization.

Russia has presumably solved the problem of justice and security in the realm of economic life; but she has paid a high price for the solution in the loss of political liberties. The totalitarian aspects of the Russian régime obscure the genuine achievements of Russian equalitarianism; and give the privileged classes of the western community the occasion to identify falsely political liberty in general with the anachronistic liberty of the economic oligarchy in capitalistic society. If economic power is not brought under more effective social and political restraint, it may well destroy the securities of the common people to the point of undermining the very fabric of western civilization. Of the great powers, Britain is most likely to solve this problem without the loss of democratic liberties; and America is most likely to make abortive efforts to return to a "free enterprise" system, which is incompatible with the requirements of justice in a highly interdependent world.

The rise of modern fascism was partly occasioned by the inability of western civilization to solve the problem of economic justice. Fascism grew in the soil of social chaos and insecurity; and its coerced unity was an effort of modern nations, rent by class conflict, to avoid the disintegration of their national life. The cure proved worse than the disease. The terrible price which nations paid for neglecting to solve their problem of domestic justice might well have been a warning to the privileged classes of the western world. They have chosen rather to identify any effort at a real cure with this false cure; and to lay the charge of fascism against all efforts of the community to bring economic power under control.

There is something more than mere ignorance in this stupidity. It is also a form of the "vain imagination" which distinguishes sin from ignorance. The pride and power of position insinuates itself into the political judgments of the privileged. It insinuates itself into all judgments; but those who have great treasure are obviously more tempted than those who have less: "Where your treasure is, there will your heart be also." The strength to bring forth a more just social order depends partly upon the ability of the poor to transmute their resentments into genuine instruments of justice; and partly upon the ability of the rich to moderate the stupidity of sinful pride and arrogant defiance of the inevitable.

IV

Since the moral and spiritual resources to achieve a just and stable society in global terms are not yet available, we must be prepared to live for decades, and possibly for centuries, in heart-breaking frustrations, somewhat eased by small advances toward the desired goal.

It will not be easy to live in this age between the ages without being tempted to despair. Richer resources of faith will be required than those which the liberal culture of the past two centuries has lived by. Its faith grew out of an age of easy achievements and few frustrations; and has little conception of the tragic character of history.

These resources can not be enlarged upon here, but two facets of an adequate faith for our age between the ages must be mentioned. The one is a form of hope which gives meaning to life not only by what is accomplished in history. We can not live by historic achievement alone, though we can not live meaningfully without historic achievement. The Christian faith has been at a discount in recent centuries because its confidence that "neither life nor death can separate us from the love of God" seemed a desperate kind of hope which was irrelevant to the needs of men who found all their hopes easily fulfilled in history. There are periods of historic achievement in the life of mankind, just as there are periods of fulfillment in the lives of individuals, when the problem of frustration does not arise as a serious issue. But there are also periods when our hopes so far exceed our grasp that we can not count on historic fulfillments to give completion to our life.

There must be a new appreciation of the meaning of the words of St. Paul that "if in this life only we have hope in Christ, we are of all men most miserable." Without the understanding of this depth of human existence it will be difficult to traverse the age between the ages.

The other resource required for our day is a sense of humility which recognizes the lack of strength to bring forth as a common form of human weakness in which all share. We must avoid the peril of attributing our historic frustration to this or that nation—to Russian intransigeance, or "British imperialism," or American pride, or any one of the specific forms which the spiritual inadequacies of our day will take. The temptation to do this will be great because there will be many explicit and unique forms of spiritual failure in our day in this class and that nation. It will be necessary to define and isolate these special forms of social and political failure and to deal with their specific causes. But it is equally important to recognize the common root of the failure of all the nations, lest a combination of our pride and our frustration lead to intolerable resentments toward each other.

Human beings in general are more tragic in their stupidities than we have generally believed; and their stupidities are derived from vain imaginations which only great suffering can eradicate. All our new births are brought about in pain; and the pain and sorrow of re-birth are greater than the pain of natural birth.

The periods of gestation for the births of history are, moreover, very long; so long that they try our patience and tempt us to believe that history is sterile. This is not the case. Mankind will finally find political instruments and moral resources adequate for a wholesome communal life on a world-wide scale. But generations and centuries may be required to complete the task.

IV

THE NEMESIS OF NATIONS

"And it came to pass in the eleventh year, in the third month, in the first day of the month, that the word of the Lord came unto me, saying, Son of man, say unto Pharaoh king of Egypt, and to his multitude; Whom art thou like in thy greatness? Behold, the Assyrian was a cedar in Lebanon with fair branches, and with a shadowing shroud, and of high stature; and his top was among the thick boughs. The waters made him great, the deep set him up on high with her rivers running round about his plants; and sent out her little rivers unto all the trees of the field. Therefore his height was exalted above all the trees of the field, and his boughs were multiplied, and his branches became long because of the multitude of waters, when he shot forth. All the fowls of heaven made their nests in his boughs, and under his branches did all the beasts of the field bring forth their young; and under his shadow dwelt all great nations. Thus was he fair in his greatness, in the length of his branches: for his root was by great waters. The cedars in the garden of God could not hide him: the fir trees were not *like his boughs, and the chestnut trees were like his branches; nor any tree in the garden of God was like unto him in his beauty. I have made him fair by the multitude of his branches: so that all the trees of Eden, that were in the garden of God, envied him.*

"Therefore thus said the Lord God; Because thou hast lifted up thyself in height, and he hath shot up his top among the thick boughs, and his heart is lifted up in his height: I have therefore delivered him into the hand of the mighty one of the heathen; he shall surely deal with him; I have driven him out for his wickedness. And strangers, the terrible of the nations, have cut him off, and have left him: upon the mountains and in all the valleys his branches are broken, and his boughs are broken by all the rivers of the land; and all the people of the earth are gone down from his shadow, and have left him. Upon his ruin shall all the fowls of the heaven remain, and all the beasts of the field shall be upon his branches: To the end that none of all the trees by the waters exalt themselves for their height, neither shoot up their top among the thick boughs, neither their trees stand up in their height, all that drink water: for they are all delivered unto death, to the nether parts of the earth, in the midst of the children of men, with them that go down to the pit."
Ezek. 31:1-14.

This parable of the trees is one of a series of judgments upon the nations which the prophet Ezekiel proclaimed in the name of God. It was one of the distinctive aspects of Hebraic prophecy that it did not think of the judgment of God as resting primarily upon the enemies and competitors of Israel. For the prophets the divine judgment fell first of all upon Israel, the chosen nation. "You only have I known of all the families of the earth," declares the prophet Amos in the name of the Lord, "therefore I will punish you for all your iniquities." But the prophetic idea of judgment became more and more universal and the whole of history was regarded as moving under God's providence. Under this providence each of the nations could, upon occasion, become the instrument of God's designs in history, even if, as in the case of Persia under Cyrus, it was not consciously seeking to perform God's will.

However, each of the nations would also, in turn, fall under the divine condemnation. The cause of this condemnation was always the same. They exalted themselves above measure, and engaged in pretensions which exceeded the bounds of human mortality. Thus Ezekiel proclaims the judgment of God upon Tyre, "Because thine heart is lifted up, and thou hast said, I am a God, I sit in the seat of God, in the midst of the seas; yet thou art a man, and not God;—thine heart is lifted up because of thy riches,—behold, therefore, I will bring strangers upon thee, the terrible of the nations: and they shall draw their swords against the beauty of thy wisdom, and they shall defile thy brightness. They shall bring thee down to the pit. . . . Wilt thou yet say before him that slayeth thee, I am God? but thou shalt be a man, and no God, in the hand of him that slayeth thee."[1]

The prophetic judgments against the nations are always prompted by their pride, which seeks to hide the common human frailty of all achievements and constructions of men, or which denies the divine source of their power and pretends that their position among the nations is due altogether to their own achievements. Thus in the parable of our text, Assyria is compared to a tree which grows by the waters and "the waters made him great, the deep set him up on high"; but the nation forgot that it was the providence of God which made him "fair in his greatness, in the length of his branches." The nation will therefore be delivered to judgment "To the end that none of all the trees by the waters exalt themselves for their height"—nor that the mighty ones "stand up in their height—for they are all delivered unto death."

In the case of Egypt, a civilization which rested upon the fecundity produced by the Nile's periodic overflow, the pride takes the form of assuming that what has been given it as a special gift of grace is really its own achievement, and therefore belongs

---

[1] Ezek. 28:2, 5, 7, 8, 9.

completely to itself. The divine judgment runs: "Behold, I am against thee, Pharaoh king of Egypt, the great dragon that lieth in the midst of his rivers, which hath said, My river is mine own, and I have made it for myself. But I will put hooks in thy jaws . . . And I will leave thee thrown into the wilderness."[2]

The theme which underlies the prophetic judgment upon the nations is thus the idea that "nemesis" overtakes the nations because mortal men contend against God. They seek to make themselves stronger than mortal men have a right to be; and they pretend to be wiser than mortal men are. They come thus in conflict with the divine prerogatives. It may take a long while, but in the end the Divine Avenger humbles these human pretensions and brings all false majesties of history "into the pit" "to the end that none of all the trees by the waters exalt themselves for their height."

This theme is not confined to the prophets. It is one of the basic themes of the Bible. In the Genesis myth of the Fall it is suggested that false pride lies at the foundation of human sin. Man sought to penetrate to the final mystery of the "tree of the knowledge of good and evil," which, alone among the trees of the garden, was forbidden to him. That was the cause of his Fall. In the profound parable of the Tower of Babel, we are told that men sought to build

[2] Ezek. 29:3-5.

a structure "whose top may reach unto heaven," and "make us a name." God is pictured as jealous of this human effort, declaring "now nothing will be restrained from them, which they have imagined to do." Therefore he confounded their language and "scattered them abroad from thence upon the face of all the earth." [3]

Nor does the New Testament lack the same interpretation of the ultimate issue between man and God. St. Paul defines sin as man's effort to change "the glory of the uncorruptible God into an image made like to corruptible man" [4] and in his second letter to the Corinthians he defines the warfare of Christians as "casting down imaginations, and every high thing that exalteth itself against the knowledge of God, and bringing into captivity every thought to the obedience of Christ." [5] There is thus in biblical thought in general a perpetual theme of warning to men and nations "not to think of themselves more highly than they ought to think." These warnings express the uneasiness of the human soul, when informed by a profound faith, over the tendency of man to hide his weakness with a false show of strength; or to forget his limitations in the knowledge of his real, yet always limited, strength. This uneasiness is accomplished by a sense of judgment and doom. It is felt that ultimately any man or nation who seeks to usurp the place of God will be brought low. The ultimate majesty

[3] Gen. 11:4, 6, 8.   [4] Rom. 1:23.   [5] II Cor. 10:5.

which rules the world will be able to subdue all false majesties. God, who is the Creator and Judge of the whole of life, has the power to put down any rebellion of the various parts of life which make themselves into the whole. In the judgments of the prophet Ezekiel, of which our text is one, the justification for the various judgments upon the various proud nations is always that in "that day" of judgment "they may know that I am the Lord."

II

This theme of the contest between a jealous God and the pride and pretension of men is not limited to biblical thought. It is a recurring motif in Greek tragedy. The very word NEMESIS, which is generally used to describe the fate of arrogance, is derived from Greek thought. Nemesis is the consequence of pride (HYBRIS). The theme is most explicitly presented in the Promethean myth, though not confined to it. Prometheus was, it will be remembered, the demi-god who aroused the jealousy of Zeus by teaching men the use of fire. In Greek tragedy the heroes are warned again and again (frequently by words spoken by the chorus) not to arouse the anger of Zeus by attempting feats which are beyond the limit of mortal men, or by making pretensions which are in conflict with the pride of Zeus.

There is one significant difference between the

manner in which this theme is handled in Greek tragedy and its development in biblical thought. In Greek drama we are never quite certain whether Zeus's jealousy is an unwarranted divine egotism, seeking to prevent men from developing their full capacities for the sake of preserving the unchallenged character of the divine power, or whether it is the justified anger of the guardian of the whole against the anarchic pretensions of the various parts of life. Sophocles seems to come nearest to the perception of the biblical idea that the jealousy of Zeus is not some unwarranted divine caprice, but the expression of the power of ultimate order against those vitalities of life which seek to make themselves the false center of that order.

This ambivalence of Greek tragedy would seem at first blush to take the complexity of the human situation into account more adequately than the biblical account. It would seem particularly to do justice to the fact that all human powers and all extensions of these powers are creative, as well as destructive. The taming of fire was a necessary step in human civilization; and Zeus's anger against Prometheus would therefore seem to be unjustified. The "knowledge of good and evil" is a necessary expression of the final "freedom of the human spirit" and the building of towers "whose top may reach into heaven" is a necessary expression of the human skill which has raised man from complete dependence upon nature to a relative mastery of nature.

The extension of human powers is the basis of the progressive character of human history. Every new conquest of nature and every new elaboration of human skills means that human actions and responsibilities are set in the context of a wider field. This is the creative side of human history. Yet every new mastery of nature and every enlargement of human powers is also the new occasion for pride and a fresh temptation to human arrogance. If biblical thought seems to neglect the creative aspect of the extension of human powers in its prophecies of doom upon proud nations, this is due only to the fact that it is more certain than is Greek thought that, whatever the creative nature of human achievements, there is always a destructive element in human power. The Bible is so certain of this because it is more certain of the majesty of God and more sure of the justice of His jealousy. It is certain that there is one God, and that "it is he that hath made us and not we ourselves," and that His majesty transcends all human majesties. It is also certain that all human majesties and powers claim a more central position in the scheme of things than is their rightful due. It understands, in other words, the tragedy of sin without denying the creative character of human achievements. It knows that jealousy of God is not the caprice of one life in competition with other life. It is rather the justice of the Lord of life against the pretentious attempts of little forms of life "To the end that none of all the trees by the waters exalt themselves for their height,"—nor that the mighty ones "stand up in their height—for they are all delivered unto death."

III

Living in an age of atomic energy and of total wars, it seems almost fantastic to think that men of any other age should have considered the perils of human pride and the temptations of human power. There were, to be sure, great empires in those days; and their rulers claimed divine majesty. But these ancient civilizations, resting upon a simple agrarian economy, were infantile in their strength compared to the power which modern men and nations have achieved through the technics of modern civilization. If the human situation warranted the warnings of the prophets in those days, how much more are those warnings justified in our day! There is in fact no greater proof of the perennial relevance of the biblical analysis of the meaning of life than that the course of history seems to make it ever more true. While our modern culture rested upon the assumption that the elaboration of human powers would be almost exclusively creative and would guarantee the achievement of ever wider and more inclusive human communities, our modern civilization produced an atomic bomb—the first effect of which can only be to sharpen the conflict of nations and to tempt nations to new forms of pride and arrogance. The atomic bomb is the most telling proof of the perpetual relevance of the biblical warnings; and even of their ever-increasing relevance as human powers increase, while the essential finiteness of the agents who wield these powers does not change.

The most immediate relevance of the prophetic promise of doom upon the trees that "exalt themselves for their height" is, of course, the ignominious end of proud dictators and "master" races, who sought only yesterday to enthrall the world and who are today completely humiliated and defeated. In one fateful week of the year 1945, one dictator died an obscene death in expiation for an obscenely ambitious life; and another died in the violence which his life had breathed. Whatever the sins of other nations, those nations were still good enough to be executors of divine judgment upon the impossible pretensions of power of these dictators and of the nations who had followed their beguilements. We are not wrong if we sense, beyond and above the purely political dimensions of the drama of these years, a deeper and more divine dimension. One can almost hear God speaking through Ezekiel to these nations: "Wilt thou yet say before him that slayeth thee, I am God? but thou shalt be a man, and no God, in the hand of him that slayeth thee."

The most obvious relevance of the biblical conception of the contest between God and man is thus the explicit doom which has descended upon nations which have most explicitly defied the proper limits of all human agencies which "are all delivered unto death," and which have tried most idolatrously to usurp the place of the divine. Yet it would be very superficial to apply this prophecy of judgment only to our enemies. We do well to remember how great the power of the victorious nations is, and what temptations lurk in the possession of this power.

We did not contrive, as the Nazis did, to bring other nations completely in our power; but we do well to consider that the defeated nations are, in fact, in our power; and that the possession of absolute power is a peril to justice.

No man or nation is wise or good enough to hold the power which the great nations in the victorious alliance hold without being tempted to both pride and injustice. Pride is the religious dimension of the sin which flows from absolute power; and injustice is its social dimension. The great nations speak so glibly of their passion for justice and peace; and so obviously betray interests which contradict justice and peace. This is precisely the kind of spiritual pride which the prophets had in mind when they pronounced divine judgment upon the nations which said, "I am god, I sit in the seat of God." Consider how blandly the victorious nations draw plans for destroying the economic and political life of defeated nations in the hope of rebuilding them as democracies "from the ground up." This lack of consideration for the organic aspects of the social existence of other nations, this confidence in our ability to create something better by our fiat, is a perfect illustration of the pride of power. It is not made any more sufferable by the idea that we are doing all this for the sake of "purging" the defeated nations of their evil and bestowing our "democracy" upon them. The very absurdity of bestowing democracy by the will of the conqueror contains the pretension against which the prophets inveighed.

IV

But neither the doom which has already fallen upon the pride of dictators, nor the impending doom which must fall upon the pride of the victors, is the most obvious point of relevance between the biblical theme of the contest between God and man and the experience of our own day. The most obvious point of relevance lies in the fact that several centuries of technical achievement have been crowned with the discovery of methods for releasing atomic energy. This new discovery crowns the creative achievements of a technical society which has increased man's mastery of nature immeasurably and which has enhanced the power of all human vitalities. But the new discovery also crowns the pretensions of modern civilization; it gives man a power which obscures his weakness. And it is a dangerous new power precisely because it is given to some men and some nations who are actually in competition with other nations; but who will seek by this power to place themselves above this competition.

The contradiction between the greatness of the power in the hands of modern men and nations, and the weakness and mortality of the agencies which wield the power, is commonly interpreted as a contradiction between the perfection of the natural sciences and the imperfection of the social sciences; or as a contrast between the scientific and the moral achievements of men. But these contrasts are due to something more than a cultural lag. They reach down to the very paradox of human existence: the greatness and the weakness of man. This paradox becomes progressively more dangerous because man's powers are continually increasing and yet man's essential weakness remains the same.

A nation which has the power to annihilate other nations does not achieve, as a concomitant of that power, the transcendent wisdom which would make it the safe custodian of such power. The possession of this power by a group of nations has the immediate prospects of peace because it will make other nations reluctant to challenge the possessors. Yet there are no ultimate promises of peace in the possession of such power by a nation or a group of nations; because other nations will resent this exclusive possession; will rightly or wrongly question the justice of the policies which are dictated by it; and will seek to come into the possession of the same power or of some other secret equally potent and dangerous.

Ultimately, of course, the increase in the power of human destructiveness must make for the organization of the world community. The destructive power has become so great that it threatens the nations with mutual annihilation. It may be, therefore, that the fear of such annihilation will persuade them to moderate their pride and their inclination to cling to the momentary advantages of the possession of disproportionate power. Whether this will be accomplished before men taste, even more than they have done, the terror of modern warfare; whether they must be brought to the very brink of disaster before they will seek to bring great power under the agency of the most impartial instruments of government which human ingenuity can devise, depends upon the degree to which they sense and anticipate the NEMESIS which threatens all human pretensions.

The point of the prophetic anticipations of doom was always partly to avoid the doom by inducing a humble and contrite anticipation of it. There are always possibilities of "fleeing the wrath which is to come." Our generation has been given such a possibility even as it is confronted with a kind of wrath more terrible than that faced by previous generations.

The kind of humility which is required of the nations to meet the possession of the new powers in their possession may be partly achieved by a shrewd political intelligence, which is able to measure the probable effect of certain policies upon attitudes of other nations. It is possible, for instance, for a shrewd political observer to know in advance that the display of power by a single nation or group of nations can not permanently secure the acquiescence of other nations. But ultimately this humility is a religious achievement. Rather it is not so much an achievement as it is a gift of grace, a by-product of the faith which discerns life in its total dimension and senses the divine judgment which stands above and against all human judgments; and of the divine majesty which is justifiably jealous of human pretensions. The more men and nations fear the wrath of God, the more can they be brought under the sway of the divine mercy. The more they anticipate doom, the more can they avoid it.

V

THE CITY WHICH HATH FOUNDATIONS

"By faith Abraham, when he was called to go out into a place which he should after receive for an inheritance, obeyed; and he went out, not knowing whither he went. By faith he sojourned in the land of promise, as in a strange country, dwelling in tabernacles with Isaac and Jacob, the heirs with him of the same promise: For he looked for a city which hath foundations, whose builder and maker is God." Heb. 11:8-10.

F ROM the perspective of modern culture the Christian faith is "other-worldly," entertaining hopes of human fulfillment beyond all historic possibilities. The eighteenth and nineteenth centuries assumed that if only these other-worldly hopes, which seemed to beguile man from his mundane tasks, could be disavowed it would be possible to center human attention so completely upon the achievement of the "land of promise" in this world that all of man's frustrations could be overcome. Actually the faith of the Bible, as compared with the other-worldliness of either the classical western age or the Orient, is stubbornly "this-worldly" from the day of the Messianic expectations of the prophets to the prayer of Christ: "thy Kingdom come, thy will be done on earth as it is in heaven."

Yet the faith of the Bible is never purely this-worldly. The Messianic hope of the prophets was an interesting mixture of historic and trans-historic expectations. In one sense the Messianic kingdom would be the completion and fulfillment of history; and in another sense it would be the end of history. The fulfillments which the prophets expected could not be contained within the limits of the historic enterprise, as it is rooted in time-nature and as it is circumscribed by the conditions of finite existence. This combination of this-worldly and other-worldly hopes is the only adequate religious expression of the human situation. For man's freedom over nature and his capacity to make history mean that there are indeterminate possibilities of historic fulfillment of human hopes; but this freedom also means that man finally transcends the whole historic process in the ultimate reaches of his spirit. There are no historic possibilities which meet the final definitions of realized goodness which are implicit in the life of spirit. Biblical faith is thus both this-worldly and other-worldly; but in Christian history the two emphases tend always to become separated, so that various ages are tempted to center their attention too much upon either the one or the other.

There is no nicer expression of the delicate biblical balance between the two facets of hope than in the words of our text in the eleventh chapter of the Epistle to the Hebrews. The whole chapter deals with the power of religious hope and faith, the two being equated in the introductory words: "Now faith is the substance of things hoped for, the evidence of things not seen." The various achievements of the prophets and martyrs of the ages are recounted, who lived and moved in the power of faith, and by that power "subdued kingdoms, wrought righteousness, obtained promises, stopped the mouths of lions, quenched the violence of fire, escaped the edge of the sword, . . . waxed valiant in fight, turned to flight the armies of aliens." On the whole the attention seems to be directed toward the possibility of "obtaining promises" in this world by the courage which faith induces. Yet there is a subtle interweaving of the other hope which is directed toward a redemption beyond history. The relation of the two hopes is beautifully expressed in the symbolism of our text.

The story of Abraham's special call from God and his finding the "promised land" was the very foundation of the historical self-consciousness of the Hebrew people. It was by that call to Abraham that they became an elect people; and the attainment of the land of promise was the legendary expression of their sense of national origin, just as the hope of the reclamation of the same promised land remained, and still is, the expression of their sense of final national salvation. It is therefore a perfect symbol of the kind of historical hope which all nations have in varying degrees, though not always in as overt religious terms as the Israelites.

But the author of the epistle introduces another note in the account of Abraham's venture which makes explicit what lies implicit in the whole prophetic interpretation of the "land of promise." Abraham, he declares, when he had attained the land of promise, lived there with his heirs in "tents" or "tabernacles," thereby signifying that he was a "stranger" in it, that he had no abiding place there, and that he looked for something more secure than any earthly land of promise, for a "city which hath foundations, whose builder and maker is God."

This poetic reinterpretation of what was to begin with a legendary account is done with a poetic touch. Abraham symbolized the pastoral period of history; and the movement toward Canaan signifies the development from pastoral to agrarian life. If Abraham did indeed continue to live in tents, that would mean that pastoral modes of life had not yet yielded to the more stable forms of abode characteristic of an agrarian society. Pastoral peoples were always "strangers" and wanderers, moving from pasture to pasture. This insecurity of a pre-agrarian period is thus re-interpreted by the writer as signifying a more ultimate insecurity. Abraham lived in tents, he declared, because he regarded himself a "stranger" in the very land which was promised him. He was strange in it because he looked beyond the earthly land of promise to a more ultimate security in a city "which hath foundations whose builder and maker is God."

This is a poetic expression of the human situation. The faith of all men and nations drives them toward the "land of promise"—toward the hope of an historic fulfillment in which the "slavery" of Egypt is overcome, independence is established and preserved against the threats of the more powerful adjacent nations. Men seek both freedom and brotherhood in human history. The earthly hope of Israel included both the establishment and preservation of national independence and the achievement of a real brotherhood of nations, with "Zion" as the center of this Messianic reign of peace and goodwill.

There are elements of hope and faith analogous to this expectation in the life of modern nations. The recently occupied and enslaved nations of Europe all hope for a renaissance of their national existence; and most of them are dimly aware of the necessity of a higher form of brotherhood between them if their independence is to have any stability and their life any fulfillment. Not the nations only which have suffered something analogous to the Egyptian slavery look forward to a new fulfillment of their life in the future. Even the strong and great nations have their special expectations. Some idea of national aggrandizement is mixed with these hopes. No nation is so strong and great that it does not think of some way of rounding out its power and security. But on the whole the hopes of the nations of the world, in the present historic situation, emphasize the ideal of peace and brotherhood. Whatever may be the special hope of each nation for the achievement of this security or that prestige, for emancipation from this usurpation or for surmounting of that weakness, all have been prompted by the ravages of two world wars to look forward to the possibility of a more stable security and the creation of a peaceful world order.

Just as nationalistic and universalistic elements were present in the Messianic expectations of even the greatest of the prophets, so also now each nation mixes a certain degree of egotistic corruption with its more generous hopes. Thus Americans hope not only for a reign of peace but also for an "American century," while Russians hope for the realization of a communist world society and also for a world-political situation in which Russian power and pride will be established; and Britain combines its desire for world brotherhood with the hope that its imperial system may not be too much at a disadvantage in comparison with the power of its partners. These nationalistic overtones and undertones are never absent; yet they do not obscure the more generous hope for the establishment of a world community in which all nations may share. This is the "promised land" of the nations, whatever the private and peculiar "promised land" of each may be.

II

This international expectation is obviously one dimension of the meaning of our life in this era. It defines our moral and social responsibilities in the most inclusive terms. It points to the obvious line which historic development must take. It rightly assumes that there are possibilities in history of making actual, what is potential; for the world community has been made potential by the development of a technical civilization in which all the nations have been brought into intimate contact with each other. It must be made actual by the development of political institutions in which the partnership of nations and their peaceful accord with each other will become real.

The proponents of eighteenth- and nineteenth-century this-worldliness may plausibly argue that our present situation, with all its urgencies and possibilities, is ample proof of the necessity and possibility of disavowing all expectations of a more eternal city, and of centering our hopes in the earthly city, or more particularly in the generous universal transfiguration of the hope of the earthly city into a city "which lies four-square," into which the peoples of the world may enter from east and west, from north and south.

Yet it is precisely in our present historic situation, when more profoundly considered, that the justification for, and the validity of, the more supernal hope is found. While the meaning of our existence lies partly in the hope of fulfilling the promises of a universal community which are implicit in the whole human adventure, we must also be prepared for the frustration of these hopes to a very considerable degree. The difficulty of religions which limit their hopes to historic possibilities is that they tempt men to despair when the possibilities are not fulfilled.

The coming decades, and indeed the coming centuries, will be characterized by frustrations as well as by fulfillments. The resources for the establishment of a universal community are not adequate. Every previous larger community of mankind has been held together partly by forces of nature and destiny, by consanguinity and a common language, by geographic boundaries, common traditions, and the memories of common experiences. The universal community has only two minimal forces making for its unity. The one is the force of fear that failure to achieve unity will involve us in universal chaos. The other is the religious and moral sense of an obligation more universal than the partial loyalties which bind our national and imperial communities together. Between the force of fear and the sense of universal brotherhood, the universal community lacks the intermediate forces of togetherness which national communities possess in their common language, culture and tradition.

These inadequacies are so important that we can not be altogether certain whether a universal community of real stability can be established. It may be that the invention of the atomic bomb will so increase the fear of future wars that what now seems impossible will become possible. Yet the fear of war is never as strong a unifying force in history as the fear of a common foe, which has played a part in the unification of all larger communities. The fear of war as such may well prompt all nations to desire a system of universal justice; but it will hardly prevent the greater powers from each seeking for themselves special advantages in such a system incompatible with the security of the whole.

If one considers the power impulses of the great nations and empires and remembers that the pride of these nations has been enhanced, rather than mitigated, by recent history, one may well wonder how a moral and political force at the center of a world community can be constructed, powerful enough to coerce, and with sufficient moral and political prestige to gain, the willing obedience of the great nations. Undoubtedly many of these difficulties will be overcome in the course of time. But it is not likely that they will be overcome so completely that a perfectly stable and harmonious universal state will be created. We have probably reached a level of historic development where even indeterminate historical possibilities can not hide certain ultimate frustrations. Mr. Mortimer Adler [1] predicts that a universal state will possibly be achieved after five hundred years of trial and error when it will finally become apparent that the kind of alliances into which the nations are now entering after this war are not adequate for the preservation of permanent peace. But he takes upon himself to guarantee that the ultimate creation of such a state will furnish the final certainty of perpetual peace. Since no lesser human community, national or imperial, has an absolutely stable harmony, and since all historic achievements of coordination and cooperation must partially suppress, rather than resolve, competing interests, this is a rather bold guarantee, and one which history will probably not justify.

Our era of historic development is therefore destined to experience both important realizations of hopes and equally significant frustrations. Some of the frustrations will be overcome in due time, though we are not the generation which will experience the significant fulfillment. We are therefore a generation which must have the spiritual resources to deal with the problem of frustration.

[1] *How to Think About War and Peace.*

III

We must consider, however, that an epoch which is confronted with the ultimate task of the human community may also, if it views its situation profoundly, recognize not merely the immediate frustrations to which it is subject but also the final disappointments to which all ages must adjust themselves. If we regard the difficulties of achieving a universal community as merely momentary, it will be possible of course to live by a hope which is prepared patiently to wait for deferred fulfillments. Moses was not the first or the last leader, seeking a land of promise, who perished outside its borders. There are indeed so many possibilities of achieving tomorrow what lies beyond the range of possibility today that a secular religion, such as prevails in our culture, can and will keep its strength for some time to come by imagining that every tomorrow will finally solve, not only the unsolved problems of today, but also the insoluble problems of history.

But no profound analysis of the human situation can justify such an interpretation of man's historic tasks and possibilities. A deeper probing of our problem must inevitably lead to the conclusion that frustration is as permanent an aspect of human existence as realization. Man's search for a "city which hath foundations, whose builder and maker is God" is occasioned by the fact that the freedom of the human spirit finally transcends all limits of nature. The good which man must claim as his final goal rises above all historic possibilities. Historic achievements are not merely limited by the conditions which nature-history sets, but are also corrupted by the pride which man in his freedom may introduce into the achievements of history.

The particular task of creating a universal community which faces our age is the most vivid portrayal of the limits, as well as the possibilities, of history. We face the task of creating a world-wide community precisely because man is too free to recognize any boundaries of nature as the final limits of his obligation to his fellowmen. Moreover his technical skills constantly enlarge or defy those boundaries. That freedom is the basis of the whole historical development which finally culminates in the task of creating community in world-wide terms. On the other hand this same man is bound to this or that place, speaks a particular language, and has organic ties with a portion of his fellowmen but not with all of them. In the words of Kipling:

> "God gave all men all earth to love,
> But, since our hearts are small,
> Ordained for each one spot should prove
> Beloved over all."

The tension between what is particular and what is universal in man is not confined to any one age, though it may be more clearly revealed in some epochs than in others. It is a permanent tension in human history. The "city of God" is consistently conceived by all great prophets as a universal community in which no distinctions of race or geography are known. Yet every city of man, no matter how great its achievements, makes such distinctions.

These distinctions are the marks of natural finiteness. They are transmuted into more stubborn and positive handicaps to the achievement of the universal by the false visions of the universal which arise in them. This false element is the factor of "sin" in the human situation. Our racial tensions, for instance, are not merely the frictions of ignorance. They are made particularly tragic because each race and group, with partly conscious and partly unconscious perversity, pretends to embody the final form of human virtue or beauty or manliness; and condemns the other groups for their failure to conform to this absolute standard. Mixed with every effort toward unity, including the unity of religious denominations, is the belief that the enlarged common life must conform to our particular pattern of life on the supposition that our pattern conforms most nearly to the absolute one. The reunion of Christian denominations is, in some respects, more difficult than the unification of secular and political communities, precisely because the explicit religious element, at the center of the religious community, also lends itself to the most explicit forms of the pretensions of finality. That is why the Christian Church must be more humble and not suggest so complacently that it has achieved, in its own life, a form of universal love which it would bestow upon the nations.

One need only analyze the two facets of the hope of the promised land as it exists in every nation, and has from the days of Abraham, to know that the most perfect form of that hope is subject to historical frustration. The most perfect form is the hope of a universal community. But mixed with this hope is the idea that our nation may have some place, particularly close to the center of it, or gain some special prestige, or be in a special way the seat of authority in it. Even the greatest prophets were certain that the law of the universal community would come from "Zion." The inevitable friction between the three great centers of international power in the modern world, British, Russian and American, will be caused not simply by the naked will-to-power of each of them, but by the partly honest conviction of each that it has a better method of world organization than the others, or that its skills, experience, ideals or political virtues are superior. No promised land can be conceived by man, or at least not in the collective consciousness of a nation, without being partially corrupted by egoistic reservations. There is thus a spiritual source of corruption in the very historic projections of the ultimate goal of history which prevents history from fulfilling itself.

IV

There are modern dissenters from the Christian faith who are perfectly willing to admit that a hiatus always remains between any achieved promised land of human history and the ultimate vision of the Kingdom of God—a vision which is incidentally so implicit in the human situation that even the most secularized religions have some version of it. The great majority of dissenters do not of course acknowledge the permanency of this contradiction. They believe that the future will resolve it. But even those who do recognize this aspect of human history are not thereby persuaded that there is a "city which hath foundations, whose builder and maker is God." They accept the tragic aspects of ultimate frustration in history but they find no relief from it. They regard the pinnacles of Christian hope as either harmless, or possibly as harmful, illusions which the weak and the credulous may require but which are not necessary for the sanity of robust spirits.

Actually this vision of the Kingdom of God, offering a security and fulfillment beyond all securities and insecurities, beyond all fulfillments and frustrations in history, is not some primitive illusion or harmless vagary of the human spirit. It is the crown of faith which completes the meaning of human existence. Man, who lives both in time and beyond time, both within and beyond the limits of nature, can not complete his life within time or nature, except as he completes it falsely by projecting the peculiar and conditioned circumstances of his life into the ultimate. Man lives beyond time in the sense that time is in him, as well as he in time. His consciousness and memory hold the moments of time which he traverses in a meaningful whole; yet the meaning is constantly broken by the fact that he is immersed in the process which he thus holds within his consciousness. This paradox of human existence can not be resolved by speculation. It can be resolved only by faith. The faith which resolves it is not some simple credulity. It is the expression of the final power of the human spirit in the recognition of its final weakness. "Not that we are sufficient of ourselves," declares St. Paul, "to think any thing as of ourselves; but our sufficiency is of God." [1] This is an acknowledgement of the limits of human powers and at the same time an expression of the belief that the limits of human powers are not the limits of the meaning of existence. We are too limited either to comprehend the whole world of meaning or to complete and fulfill the meaning which we comprehend. This human situation either tempts us to despair, if it should persuade us that our inability to complete the world of meaning destroys such partial meaning as we do discern; or it prompts us to faith, if we should find the power and wisdom beyond

[1] II Cor. 3:5.

our own, in the very realization of our limited power and wisdom.

The religious community, including the Christian Church, has frequently given a certain validity to the scepticism of the dissenters from religion by filling the sense of an ultimate fulfillment of life with too specific content and by claiming to know too much about the dimensions, the geography, and the whole structure of the city of God. All visions in time of the completion of the time process, all previsions of the fulfillment of life, must remain decently humble and modest. "It doth not yet appear what we shall be." Every too specific definition becomes a bearer of some human pretension. On the whole the primary error in Christian other-worldliness has been its too consistent individualism. There is usually no suggestion of a "city of God" in them. The vision of life's fulfillment has been primarily a vision of individual completion beyond the frustrations of human communities. It has not been a vision of the fulfillment of the communal process. Thus the sceptics have frequently been the primary bearers of the social meaning of existence. Actually there are aspects of both individual and collective existence and meaning which transcend the possibilities of history. If there is a fulfillment, it must be both social and individual. This twofold aspect of human existence is well understood in Hebraic prophecy. The vision of the Messianic kingdom always implies both individual and social fulfillment.

But orthodox Christianity, both Catholic and Protestant, has frequently destroyed the idea of social and communal fulfillment; and Protestant Christianity, at least, has frequently derived this error in its final hope from a too consistent individualism in interpreting the meaning of man's present existence.

A faith which claims to know too much is not merely the bearer of the pretensions of wisdom, but also the instrument of human will-to-power. Invariably it suggests that the ultimate fulfillment of life also involves a specially advantageous completion of the projector of the vision. For this reason the scepticism of the secular world is actually a wholesome source of faith's purification. Yet such a scepticism, developed consistently, must finally arrive at the conclusion that the partial meanings of human history are too incomplete and corrupted to be meanings at all. Faith in the ultimate fulfillment of the meaning implicit in human existence is therefore primarily an assertion of the reality of that meaning.

The structure of man, for instance, is such that he can not complete himself within himself. Love and brotherhood are the law of his existence. Furthermore there are no natural limits of brotherhood. The law of love is universal. There are indeterminate possibilities of realizing a wider brotherhood in history. But the natural limits are never completely transcended. Man is never quite universal man in history; but black man and white man, European and Asiatic,

American and Russian. Furthermore each kind of man introduces the corruption of sin into this finiteness by claiming for his partial and peculiar manhood more ultimate significance than it possesses. If the transcendent reality of brotherhood is not emphasized the partial and corrupted definitions of man, as we have them in history, can become perversely normative as they did in Nazism. The liberal democratic world saved itself from this perversity by the hope of a complete historical realization of universal man. Future ages are bound to invalidate this hope. It is at that point that the issue between the Christian faith in the "city which hath foundations" and moral cynicism will become fully joined.

V

We must consider in conclusion the not unjustified feeling of modern proponents of "this-worldliness" that the vision of the "city which hath foundations" beguiles men from seeking the promised lands of human history. No one can deny that Christian otherworldliness has frequently beguiled men from achieving higher possibilities in history. There is a form of Christian moral cynicism which believes, for instance, that Christian universalism is not to be fulfilled in history because it will be ultimately fulfilled; that the dictum of St. Paul that in "Christ there is neither Jew nor Greek" applies to "the resurrection" and therefore not to this earth. There was a form of Nazified German Christianity which sought this way of escape from the moral obligations of Christian universalism. There are also types of Christian pessimism which will not take the task of building a peaceful world community seriously, on the ground that the Scripture prophesies "war and rumours of wars" to the end of history.

These corruptions of the Christian faith must be humbly acknowledged by the Christian community. It must be recognized that this impulse toward the achievement of justice and brotherhood in the past two centuries has frequently been borne primarily by secularists who emphasized the petition which Christians had neglected: "Thy Kingdom come, thy will be done on earth as it is in heaven."

On the other hand the secular world has not recognized to what degree its obligations to realize the historically possible have been confused by alternating illusions and disillusionments, by too facile hopes and consequent moods of despair.

Ideally there is a tremendous resource for the accomplishment of immediate possibilities in an ultimate hope. Such a hope frees us from preoccupation with the prospects of immediate success or fears of immanent failure. It helps us to do our duty without allowing it to be defined by either our hopes or our fears. This is a resource which will be particularly required in the coming decades and centuries. We do not know how soon and to what degree mankind will succeed in establishing a tolerable world order. Very possibly we will hover for some centuries between success and failure, in such a way that optimists and pessimists will be able to assess our achievements, or lack of them, with an equal degree of plausibility. In such a situation it is important to be more concerned with our duties than with the prospect of success in fulfilling them. It is not recorded that Abraham was less assiduous in seeking the promised land because of his feeling that he would be a stranger in it, once he reached it.

A sense of ultimate security and ultimate fulfillment may beguile a few from their immediate tasks. But the heroic soul will be the freer to seek for possible securities in history if he possesses a resource against immediate insecurities. The city of God is no enemy of the land of promise. The hope of it makes the inevitable disappointments in every land of promise tolerable.

VI

TODAY, TOMORROW AND THE ETERNAL

"*Take therefore no thought for the morrow: for the morrow shall take thought for the things of itself. Sufficient unto the day is the evil thereof.*" Mt. 6:34.

"*Then shall the kingdom of heaven be likened unto ten virgins, which took their lamps, and went forth to meet the bridegroom. And five of them were wise and five were foolish. They that were foolish took their lamps, and took no oil with them: But the wise took oil in their vessels with their lamps. While the bridegroom tarried, they all slumbered and slept. And at midnight there was a cry made, Behold the bridegroom cometh; go ye out to meet him. Then all those virgins arose, and trimmed their lamps. And the foolish said unto the wise, Give us of your oil; for our lamps are gone out. But the wise answered, saying, Not so; lest there be not enough for us and you; but go ye rather to them that sell, and buy for yourselves. And while they went to buy, the bridegroom came; and they that were ready went in with him to the marriage: and the door was shut. Afterward came also the other virgins, saying, Lord, Lord open to us. But he answered and said, Verily I say unto you, I know you not. Watch therefore, for ye know neither the day nor the hour wherein the Son of man cometh."* Mt. 25:1-13.

The foolish virgins were chided because they were not prepared for the promise and opportunity of tomorrow. Yet the same Christ who uttered this parable included the admonition, "Be not anxious for tomorrow," in the Sermon on the Mount.

The parable of the Wise and Foolish Virgins is one of the Messianic or "eschatological" parables, which deals with the promised coming of the Messianic reign. Jesus consistently maintained that we must always be ready for this final fulfillment of the whole promise and meaning of life, "for ye know neither the day not the hour wherein the Son of man cometh." It is to be noted that the foolish virgins were completely shut out from the marriage feast (this feast being a traditional symbol of the final culmination of history in the reign of the Messiah). Their lack of preparedness for the critical hour seemed to have doomed them completely. There is thus a strong emphasis in the parable upon constant preparedness for the critical hour of opportunity.

This hour of opportunity has a very ultimate significance in the text; for it is identical with the culmination of all history in the reign of the Messiah. As most biblical symbols dealing with the eternal fulfillment of the course of history, the "end of history" in the Messianic reign must not be taken literally. It must nevertheless be taken seriously because it indicates the eternal dimension in which history moves. There are moments in history which are more than mere historic moments; for in them a whole course of history is fulfilled. In them the seeming chaos of the past achieves its meaning; and the partial and particular aspects of life are illumined to become parts of a complete whole.

These moments of illumination and fulfillment have, however, no meaning at all to those who are not prepared for them. Christ does not come to those who do not expect him. The great crises of both our individual and our collective lives do not round out and complete the fragmentary character of our previous history, if that previous history is not understood as containing within itself partial meanings which are moving toward the completer revelation of their essential character. The foolish virgins are shut out of the marriage feast, and the "unlit lamp and the ungirt loin" always result in unfulfilled promises.

Yet on the other hand we have the explicit prohibition of anxiety for the morrow; and the reason given is that "sufficient unto the day is the evil thereof." There seems thus to be a contradiction between the advice to regard each day as complete in itself and the warning to be prepared for the unexpected fulfillment and completion of the tasks and events of today in an unknown tomorrow.

This seeming contradiction is occasioned by measuring two different dimensions of the acts, responsibilities, and events, which constitute the stuff of our experience. Every such act and event has an intrinsic quality which makes it complete in itself, or rather which makes it complete if it is related to the final meaning of life as we have it in our relation to God. If we used spatial symbols we could describe this dimension as a vertical one, being constituted by the direct relation of every moment of time to the eternal, or the transection of every moment by the eternal.[1] If we speak of this quality without the presupposition of faith, we define it as the "intrinsic" quality. But there can be nothing purely intrinsic in life, since all things are related to each other. What seems intrinsic is that aspect of existence which does not wait upon some future development for its meaning, but has that meaning, not within itself, but within itself in relation to what is felt to be the ultimate source of the meaning of our life.

On the other hand all life is in a moving process, and every event and act is related to future events and possibilities in which they are rounded out and fulfilled. In the Epistle to the Hebrews the author, after recounting the heroic deeds of martyrs and

[1] *Cf.* T. S. Eliot, *The Rock*.

prophets, observes that all of them "having obtained a good report, received not the promise, God having provided some better thing for us, that they without us should not be made perfect." This is to say that every generation requires its successors to complete its work. Even the most heroic and perfect action does not "receive the promise," since the fulfillment of "their" task requires "our" contribution. One thinks immediately how the dead of this war are dependent upon future generations to determine whether their sacrifice was futile or historically fruitful.

II

There is no possibility of equating these two dimensions of our existence or reducing the one to the other. Throughout our life, there is a sense in which each act and responsibility must be weighed without regard to its consequences; while from another aspect it waits for fulfillment on some tomorrow.

Consider for instance the responsibility of parents in the upbringing of children. All of these responsibilities have a vista toward the future. Each child is not what it is but what it will be; and the fond parents consider the future in the child's discipline. It is for tomorrow that this training and that preparation are undertaken. It is in the maturity of tomorrow that the care of the child finds its justification. Albert Schweitzer confesses that a strict aunt who kept him at his music lessons, when play beckoned outside, was responsible for the muscular coordination which was the basis of his skill as an organist and which could only have been acquired at an early age because the foresight of an elder counteracted childish disinclination. There is a certain pathos and yet beauty in the anxious solicitude with which parents look toward tomorrow. In a spirit of hope, mixed with apprehension, they wonder how their children will "turn out." Too much anxiety is undoubtedly harmful to the child, at least too much acknowledged anxiety. Yet it is the care of early discipline which provides the oil for the lamps for the wedding feasts of tomorrow.

But this is only one facet of the situation. Children are what they will become; but they also are what they are. A parent who did not see the perfection of childhood in each age and period which it traverses in its immaturity, and who did not recognize the meaning of his responsibility without regard to the future, would destroy one dimension of parental responsibility. There are children who do not survive to maturity. In such a situation some parents feel themselves completely defrauded. No one can deny the tragic character of a life cut off before its fruition; yet there are parents who are able to thank God in the hour of sorrow for the joy they have had in their child while they had him. Such a peace within sorrow is the fruit of faith which understands the completeness of life within each moment.

If we consider the educational preparation for life from the standpoint of the child himself, we discern the same two dimensions. The whole educational enterprise is preparation for tomorrow. Yet no young man or woman who is driven merely by ambition or the hope of being able to "make use of" the education of today can possibly enjoy study and discipline. There is an aspect of the learning adventure which makes it enjoyable and meaningful without regard to tomorrow. There is joy in trying out the wings of intellect and imagination. It is enjoyable to test growing skills of mind and to penetrate into the mysteries of life. From childhood to old age one part of the learning process is not preparation for tomorrow but an expression of the momentary spiritual capacities without regard for any tomorrow.

The cultivation of the soil is even more an obvious illustration of the two facets of experience. Every husbandman sows his seed in expectation of the fruits which it will bring forth. The justification of the sowing is in the harvest. But there are so many hazards between the sowing and the reaping that the sower might easily be tempted by his anxieties over them to shirk his task of sowing. It is well not to be too anxious about tomorrow's possible storms. "Sufficient unto the day is the evil thereof." Furthermore there are satisfactions in tilling the soil which are not drawn from the expectation of the harvest. There is satisfaction in performing one's appointed function without reference to the outcome of the task. There is joy, moreover, in the husbandman's communion with nature, in turning the fragrant earth and sensing the quiet yielding of nature's forces to the mastery of man. No one would sow, of course, if there were no reaping; if no fruits of tomorrow justify the tasks of today, these finally become meaningless. Yet the meaning of the task is not merely in tomorrow's fruition. A part of the impetus for the performing of it is derived from more immediate and yet more ultimate considerations. One does one's duty and performs one's characteristic function without too much regard for the consequences. If work were not in some sense its own reward, men would become so preoccupied with the anticipation of rewards, and with apprehensions about their possible failure, that the strength for the task would be dissipated.

III

The great experiences of the world crisis, through which we have been and are still passing, reveal the two facets of human experience. The nations of the world were faced with the threat of tyranny. Their immediate responsibility was to overcome that peril. None of the nations were too willing to accept the responsibilities which were implicit in the peril. One method of escape from the responsibility was to enlarge upon the perilous consequences of involvement in war. We were told, for instance, that we would all become fascists in our effort to destroy fascism. There was a degree of plausibility in this argument; for military discipline tends toward authoritarianism, and the high cost of war may weaken economic systems to such an extent that they may be threatened with the social chaos out of which tyrannies arise. Actually the democratic world survived, with its liberties fairly well preserved. If our anxieties for tomorrow had been our sole counsellors we should have capitulated to tyranny.

Another counsel of anxiety was the suggestion that action even against a great evil is not justified, if it has little prospect of successful conclusion. In the Catholic definition of a "just" war one of the criteria of justice enumerated is a good prospect of success. This criterion has a provisional legitimacy. Both Aristotle and Aquinas were right in suggesting that the wise man will consider whether an abortive effort to overcome an evil may not aggravate the evil. But the idea must not be pressed too consistently. One may be grateful, for instance, that Mr. Churchill did not give it any consideration in the grave hours of 1940. He would in that case have followed the course of Marshal Pétain. Mr. Churchill's greatest claim to fame, and to the respect of both his contemporaries and posterity, arises precisely from the fact that he articulated the inarticulate and yet powerful sense of a great number of his countrymen and of the civilized world, who felt that there are perils so great and responsibilities so urgent that they reduce the calculation of consequences to an irrelevance. This is an exact application of the words: "Sufficient unto the day is the evil thereof."

We have thus far dealt with the "vertical" dimension of our experience as both an obligation and an achieved task. Yet it is necessary to discriminate between the two, for the one is more absolute than the other. We may have a momentary obligation which is absolute. We perform it "in God's sight," which is to say that the responsibility is unqualified no matter how uncertain the consequences may be. In such experiences we truly measure the eternal dimension of life within its flux. On the other hand what we achieve is very imperfect, partly because the act itself is not perfect and partly because the actions of other generations are required to complete it. For this reason the sense of consummation within the relativities of life is always the part of faith. This is precisely what is meant by the biblical doctrine of "justification by faith." If we live and act in faith, the imperfections of our momentary achievements are transmuted and become a part of God's perfection. There must be forgiveness in the attitude of God toward us, for our acts are not merely imperfect, in the sense that they only approximate their ideal possibility; but there is always a positive element of evil in them. One thinks, for instance, of the degree to which national egotism and self-interest were the driving motives of the nations, prompting them to do their duty. Thus we have absolute responsibilities which represent the challenge of the eternal to our finite situation; but our achievements are only absolute by faith.

IV

But even the most superficial estimate of this "vertical" dimension of experience suggests that the more "horizontal" or historical dimension is implicit in every moment of experience. Every action is bound both to its origins and to its consequences. History is a moving stream. The completion of an act and a responsibility always lies in an historical tomorrow and not merely in the eternal.

In the present world situation it is apparent that no matter how justified we were in meeting a present peril without regard to all the historical consequences, a view of those consequences obtruded as soon as the immediate peril was less pressing. We fought to throttle tyranny in the immediate moment. But in the next moment we recognized that the tyranny grew in a soil of an international anarchy for which all nations were responsible. Thus we face the question whether we can overcome that anarchy. Can we mitigate the power of national egotism sufficiently to establish an international order?

Looked at from one aspect, the sacrifices of this

war are self-justifying, or at least they are justified by the preservation of our liberties. From another aspect they wait upon other generations for their perfecting, "God having provided some better thing for us, that they without us should not be made perfect." If this war does not issue in a more stable world order, the sacrifices which it required will have only a negative, and therefore a tragic, justification.

Whether we are able to complete the meaning of today in the achievements of tomorrow depends partly upon the degree to which we measure the meaning to today's task in depth. That is represented by the oil carried in the lamps of the wise virgins. If, for instance, an immediate peril is recognized only in its immediate dimensions, and if the deeper issues out of which it arose are not understood, we do not prepare ourselves for the more ultimate task and the more ultimate realization of our obligations. There are military minds, for instance, who insist upon viewing the present world situation in purely military and technical terms. We defeated a terrible foe, they argue, by establishing a technical supremacy over his might on land, on the sea and in the air. Our job is to maintain that supremacy under all circumstances. They regard this as an adequate preparation for the perils of the morrow. In reality this attitude represents the foolishness of the virgins, who did not realize how unexpectedly the "bridegroom" may appear tomorrow. For the Kingdom of God appears in history in every great judgment and in every new level of community. The Kingdom is always both judgment and fulfillment. In judgment the contradiction between our history and the law of God is more fully apprehended. Without this apprehension we are tempted to regard our present achievements as adequate. In the fulfillment some creative step is taken to bring our human communities into conformity with the law of brotherhood.

V

Different ages and periods of history emphasize the one or the other dimension of experience, according to their distinctive faith. Since the eighteenth century, modern culture, having lost its faith in the God who is known in Scripture, was forced to place an undue emphasis upon the fulfillments of the future as the only source of the meaning of the present. As Carl Becker has shown in his *Heavenly City of the Eighteenth Century Philosophers*, the wise men of the Enlightenment made "posterity" into the image of God. It was posterity which would judge them and find them righteous or unrighteous. It was posterity which would justify their acts by fulfilling them. The inadequacy of this faith may be discerned by the simple observation that we are the posterity to which the eighteenth century appealed and which it worshipped. Our broken and fragmentary life is hardly an adequate fulfillment of the dreams of that century; and we are much too preoccupied with our own sorrows and responsibilities to heed the outstretched hands of the eighteenth-century worshippers. We are not God. We are not even good idols. It might be observed furthermore that the eighteenth century was a very inadequate fulfillment of the faith of the seventeenth century. The conception of the meaning of life expressed in the religious controversies of the seventeenth century was profounder than was the sense of meaning in the eighteenth century. For the Enlightenment reduced everything to shallowness. We should be poor indeed if we were dependent only upon posterity to fulfill our lives. Yet there is a dimension of our existence which is fulfilled only in the future.

If the secularism of the eighteenth century gave undue emphasis to the horizontal dimension of history, orthodox Protestantism very frequently saw no significance in historical fulfillment. It believed with the great historian, Ranke, that all moments of time are equi-distant from eternity. Karl Barth, for instance, standing in the radical Reformation tradition, counselled the British Christians, in his well-known letter to them,[1] not to avail themselves of the "permission" their government had given them to discuss post-war prospects. He placed no confidence in these

[1] Karl Barth, "A Letter to Great Britain from Switzerland, April 1941," in *This Christian Cause*.

plans for the future. He placed sole emphasis upon the dimension of experience which is measured in the words, "Be not anxious for the morrow." This advice might well be contrasted with the observation of Harold Laski that if this war did not lead to a worldwide fellowship of socialist republics it would have been fought in vain. Both estimates of the present crisis are wrong because both are one-sided. Each measures only one dimension of our experience.

The two dimensions of our experience must lead to an attitude in which serenity and alertness are combined. We may be serene in the present moment, both because its obligations may have a finality which transcends the relativity of the moment, and its achievements, though imperfect, may by faith give us a sense of consummation. We must not be anxious about tomorrow, partly because we do not know tomorrow and partly because tomorrow, when known, will be less than a perfect fulfillment of our hopes. All pure instrumentalism, which judges every act and event in terms of its consequences, contains an element of pretension. It assumes that we have a more certain knowledge of future consequences than is possible for finite man, standing within the flux of time. He knows a great deal about the past, though not as much as he thinks he knows. But if his knowledge of the past is a symbol of his greatness, let him be reminded that his ignorance of the future is a sign of his weakness. If, by faith, we understand and lay hold of the divine power which completes our incompleteness, we can accept the finiteness of our life without fretfulness and anticipate every unknown tomorrow without anxiety.

And yet we shall be anxious as we look into the future. We shall survey the future with hope and apprehension. We shall survey it with apprehension because we know that there are evils in the present which must bear fruit in some terrible judgment of tomorrow. Our present apprehension must be the seed of our future repentance. We shall not know the judgment of the Kingdom of God, if apprehension does not prepare us for it. Also our present hope is the seed of our future sense of obligation. We recognize a more universal obligation emerging out of the fragmentary loyalties of today. Living in racial and national strife, and yet sensing the universal character of our obligation, we prepare ourselves to meet those obligations more full tomorrow. For the Kingdom comes in fulfillment as well as in judgment. This hope of fulfillment and this apprehension of judgment is the oil in our lamp, which helps us to enter the wedding feasts.

Only a combination of repose and anxiety, of serenity and preparedness, can do justice to the whole of our life and the whole of our world. For our life is a brief existence, moving within a great stream of finiteness. Yet the stream moves within its bed; and the flux of existence is held together by the eternal purposes of God. We ourselves stand beyond the flux in memory and hope. But we do not stand beyond it so completely that we can touch the eternal in the present moment by our own strength. We touch it by faith. That faith is the source of our serenity, even as alertness for the promises and perils of tomorrow is a reminder of our continued finiteness and sin. Both posterity and God are required to complete our life. But posterity without God would give us a very sorry completion. Wherefore even the future would become a source of intolerable anxiety if we could not believe that both tomorrow and today are in the hands of a God whose power is great enough to complete our incompleteness and whose mercy and forgiveness are adequate for the evils which we introduce into both the present and the future.

VII

HUMOUR AND FAITH

"He that sitteth in the heavens shall laugh: the Lord shall have them in derision." Ps. 2:4.

This word of the Second Psalm is the only instance in the Bible in which laughter is attributed to God. God is not frequently thought of as possessing a sense of humour, though that quality would have to be attributed to perfect personality. There are critics of religion who regard it as deficient in the sense of humour, and they can point to the fact that there is little laughter in the Bible. Why is it that Scriptural literature, though filled with rejoicings and songs of praise, is not particularly distinguished for the expression of laughter? There are many sayings of Jesus which betray a touch of ironic humour; but on the whole one must agree with the critics who do not find much humour or laughter in the Bible.

This supposed defect will, however, appear less remarkable if the relation of humour to faith is understood. Humour is, in fact, a prelude to faith; and laughter is the beginning of prayer. Laughter must be heard in the outer courts of religion; and the echoes of it should resound in the sanctuary; but there is no laughter in the holy of holies. There laughter is swallowed up in prayer and humour is fulfilled by faith.

The intimate relation between humour and faith is derived from the fact that both deal with the incongruities of our existence. Humour is concerned with the immediate incongruities of life and faith with the ultimate ones. Both humour and faith are expressions of the freedom of the human spirit, of its capacity to stand outside of life, and itself, and view the whole scene. But any view of the whole immediately creates the problem of how the incongruities of life are to be dealt with; for the effort to understand the life, and our place in it, confronts us with inconsistencies and incongruities which do not fit into any neat picture of the whole. Laughter is our reaction to immediate incongruities and those which do not affect us essentially. Faith is the only possible response to the ultimate incongruities of existence which threaten the very meaning of our life.

We laugh at what? At the sight of a fool upon the throne of the king; or the proud man suffering from some indignity; or the child introducing its irrelevancies into the conversation of the mature. We laugh at the juxtaposition of things which do not fit together. A boy slipping on the ice is not funny. Slipping on the ice is funny only if it happens to one whose dignity is upset. A favorite device of dramatists, who have no other resources of humour, is to introduce some irrelevant interest into the central theme of the drama by way of the conversation of maid or butler. If this irrelevance is to be really funny, however, it must have some more profound relation to the theme than the conversor intended. This is to say that humour manages to resolve incongruities by the discovery of another level of congruity. We laugh at the proud man slipping on the ice, not merely because the contrast between his dignity and his undignified plight strikes us as funny; but because we feel that his discomfiture is a poetically just rebuke of his dignity. Thus we deal with immediate incongruities, in which we are not too seriously involved and which open no gap in the coherence of life in such a way as to threaten us essentially. But there are profound incongruities which contain such a threat. Man's very position in the universe is incongruous. That is the problem of faith, and not of humour. Man is so great and yet so small, so significant and yet so insignificant. "On the one hand," says Edward Bellamy,[1] "is the personal life of man, an atom, a grain of sand on a boundless shore, a bubble of a foam flecked ocean, a life bearing a proportion to the mass of past, present and future, so infinitesimal as to defy the imagination. On the other hand is a certain other life, as it were a spark of the universal life, insatiable in aspiration,

[1] In *The Religion of Solidarity*.

greedy of infinity, asserting solidarity with all things and all existence, even while subject to the limitations of space and time." That is the contrast.

When man surveys the world he seems to be the very center of it; and his mind appears to be the unifying power which makes sense out of the whole. But this same man, reduced to the limits of his animal existence, is a little animalcule, preserving a precarious moment of existence within the vastness of space and time. There is a profound incongruity between the "inner" and the "outer" world, or between the world as viewed from man's perspective, and the man in the world as viewed from a more ultimate perspective. The incongruity becomes even more profound when it is considered that it is the same man who assumes the ultimate perspective from which he finds himself so insignificant.

Philosophers seek to overcome this basic incongruity by reducing one world to the dimension of the other; or raising one perspective to the height of the other. But neither a purely naturalistic nor a consistently idealistic system of philosophy is ever completely plausible. There are ultimate incongruities of life which can be resolved by faith but not by reason. Reason can look at them only from one standpoint or another, thereby denying the incongruities which it seeks to solve. They are also too profound to be resolved or dealt with by laughter. If laughter seeks to deal with the ultimate issues of life it turns into a bitter humour. This means that it has been overwhelmed by the incongruity. Laughter is thus not merely a vestibule to faith but also a "no-man's land" between faith and despair. We laugh cheerfully at the incongruities on the surface of life; but if we have no other resource but humour to deal with those which reach below the surface, our laughter becomes an expression of our sense of the meaninglessness of life.

II

Laughter is a sane and healthful response to the innocent foibles of men; and even to some which are not innocent. All men betray moods and affectations, conceits and idiosyncrasies, which could become the source of great annoyance to us if we took them too seriously. It is better to laugh at them. A sense of humour is indispensable to men of affairs who have the duty of organizing their fellowmen in common endeavors. It reduces the frictions of life and makes the foibles of men tolerable. There is, in the laughter with which we observe and greet the foibles of others, a nice mixture of mercy and judgment, of censure and forbearance. We would not laugh if we regarded these foibles as altogether fitting and proper. There is judgment, therefore, in our laughter. But we also prove by the laughter that we do not take the annoyance too seriously. However, if our fellows commit a serious offense against the common good, laughter no longer avails. If we continue to indulge in it, the element of forebearance is completely eliminated from it. Laughter against real evil is bitter. Such bitter laughter of derision has its uses as an instrument of condemnation. But there is no power in it to deter the evil against which it is directed.

There were those who thought that we could laugh Mussolini and Hitler out of court. Laughter has sometimes contributed to the loss of prestige of dying oligarchies and social systems. Thus Cervantes' *Don Quixote* contributed to the decline of feudalism, and Boccaccio's *Decameron* helped to signal the decay of medieval asceticism. But laughter alone never destroys a great seat of power and authority in history. Its efficacy is limited to preserving the self-respect of the slave against the master. It does not extend to the destruction of slavery. Thus all the victims of tyranny availed themselves of the weapon of wit to preserve their sense of personal self-respect. Laughter provided them with a little private world in which they could transvalue the values of the tyrant, and reduce his pompous power to the level of the ridiculous. Yet there is evidence that the most insufferable forms of tyranny (as in the concentration camps, for instance) could not be ameliorated by laughter.

Laughter may turn to bitterness when it faces serious evil, partly because it senses its impotence. But, in any case, serious evil must be seriously dealt with. The bitterness of derision is serious enough; but where is the resource of forgiveness to come from? It was present in the original forbearance of laughter; but it can not be brought back into the bitterness of derision. The contradiction between judgment and mercy can not be resolved by humour but only by vicarious pain.

Thus we laugh at our children when they betray the jealous conceits of childhood. These are the first buds of sin which grow in the soil of the original sin of our common humanity. But when sin has conceived and brought forth its full fruit, our laughter is too ambiguous to deal with the child's offense; or if it is not ambiguous it becomes too bitter. If we retain the original forbearance of laughter in our judgment it turns into harmful indulgence. Parental judgment is always confronted with the necessity of relating rigorous judgment creatively to the goodness of mercy. That relation can be achieved only as the parent himself suffers under the judgments which are exacted. Not humour but the cross is the meeting point of justice and mercy, once both judgment and mercy have become explicit. Laughter can express both together, when neither is fully defined. But, when it becomes necessary to define each explicitly, laughter can no longer contain them both. Mercy is expelled and only bitterness remains.

What is true of our judgments of each other is true of the judgment of God. In the word of our text God is pictured laughing at man and having him in derision because of the vanity of man's imagination and pretensions. There is no suggestion of a provisional geniality in this divine laughter. Derisiveness is pure judgment. It is not possible to resolve the contradiction between mercy and judgment, on the level of the divine, through humour; because the divine judgment is ultimate judgment. That contradiction, which remains an unsolved mystery in the Old Testament, is resolved only as God is revealed in Christ. There is no humour but suffering in that revelation. There is, as we have observed, a good deal of ironic humour in the sayings of Christ. But there is no humour in the scene of Christ upon the Cross. The only humour on Calvary is the derisive laughter of those who cried, "He saved others; himself he can not save. . . . If he be the son of God let him come down from the cross"; and the ironic inscription on the cross, ordered by Pilate: "The King of the Jews." These ironic and derisive observations were the natural reactions of common sense to dimensions of revelation which transcend common sense. Since they could not be comprehended by faith, they prompted ironic laughter.

There is no humour in the cross because the justice and the mercy of God are fully revealed in it. In that revelation God's justice is made the more terrible because the sin of man is disclosed in its full dimension. It is a rebellion against God from which God himself suffers. God can not remit the consequences of sin; yet He does show mercy by taking the consequences upon and into Himself. This is the main burden of the disclosure of God in Christ. This is the final clue to the mystery of the divine character. Mercy and justice are provisionally contained in laughter; and the contradiction between them is tentatively resolved in the sense of humour. But the final resolution of justice, fully developed, and of mercy, fully matured, is possible only when the sharp edge of justice is turned upon the executor of judgment without being blunted. This painful experience of vicarious suffering is far removed from laughter. Only an echo of the sense of humour remains in it. The echo is the recognition in the sense of humour that judgment and mercy belong together, even though they seem to be contradictory. But there is no knowledge in the sense of humour of how the two are related to each other and how the contradiction between them is to be resolved.

III

The sense of humour is even more important provisionally in dealing with our own sins than in dealing with the sins of others. Humour is a proof of the capacity of the self to gain a vantage point from which it is able to look at itself. The sense of humour is thus a by-product of self-transcendence. People with a sense of humour do not take themselves too seriously. They are able to "stand off" from themselves, see themselves in perspective, and recognize the ludicrous and absurd aspects of their pretensions. All of us ought to be ready to laugh at ourselves because all of us are a little funny in our foibles, conceits and pretensions. What is funny about us is precisely that we take ourselves too seriously. We are rather insignificant little bundles of energy and vitality in a vast organization of life. But we pretend that we are the very center of this organization. This pretension is ludicrous; and its absurdity increases with our lack of awareness of it. The less we are able to laugh at ourselves the more it becomes necessary and inevitable that others laugh at us.

It is significant that little children are really very sober though they freely indulge in a laughter which expresses a pure animal joy of existence. But they do not develop the capacity of real humour until the fifth or sixth year, at which time they may be able to laugh at themselves and at others. At about this age their intense preoccupation with self and with an immediate task at hand is partly mitigated. The sense of humour grows, in other words, with the capacity of self-transcendence. If we can gain some perspective upon our own self we are bound to find the self's pretensions a little funny.

This means that the ability to laugh at oneself is the prelude to the sense of contrition. Laughter is a vestibule to the temple of confession. But laughter is not able to deal with the problem of the sins of the self in any ultimate way. If we become fully conscious of the tragedy of sin we recognize that our preoccupation with self, our exorbitant demands upon life, our insistence that we receive more attention than our needs deserve, effect our neighbors harmfully and defraud them of their rightful due. If we recognize the real evil of sin, laughter can not deal with the problem. If we continue to laugh after having recognized the depth of evil, our laughter becomes the instrument of irresponsibility. Laughter is thus not only the vestibule of the temple of confession but the no-man's land between cynicism and contrition. Laughter may express a mood which takes neither the self nor life seriously. If we take life seriously but ourselves not too seriously, we cease to laugh. The contradiction in man between "the good that he would and does not do, and the evil that he would not do, and does" is no laughing matter.

There is furthermore another dimension in genuine contrition which laughter does not contain. It is the awareness of being judged from beyond ourselves. There is something more than self-judgment in genuine contrition. "For me it is a small thing to be judged of men," declares St. Paul, "neither judge I myself; for I know nothing against myself; he who judges me is the Lord." In an ultimate sense the self never knows anything against itself. The self of today may judge the self's action of yesterday as evil. But that means that the self of today is the good self. We are to judge our actions through self-judgment. But we do not become aware of the deep root of evil actions in such judgments. We may judge our sins but we do not judge ourselves as sinners. The knowledge that we are sinners, and that inordinate desires spring from a heart inordinately devoted to itself, is a religious knowledge which, in a sense, is never achieved except in prayer. Then we experience with St. Paul that "he who judges us is the Lord." There is no laughter in that experience. There is only pain. The genuine joy of reconciliation with God, which is possible only as the fruit of genuine repentance, is a joy which stands beyond laughter though it need not completely exclude laughter.

To suggest that the sense of humour is the beginning, but not the end, of a proper humility does not mean that the final fruit of true contrition destroys all vestiges of the seed from which it sprang. The saintliest men frequently have a humourous glint in their eyes. They retain the capacity to laugh at both themselves and at others. They do not laugh in their prayers because it is a solemn experience to be judged of God and to stand under the scrutiny of Him from whom no secrets are hid. But the absence of laughter in the most ultimate experience of life does not preclude the presence of laughter as a suffused element in all experience. There is indeed proper laughter on the other side of the experience of repentance. It is the laughter of those who have been released both from the tyranny of the law and from the slavery of pretending to be better than they are. To know oneself a sinner, to have no illusions about the self, and no inclination to appear better than we are, either in the sight of man or of God, and to know oneself forgiven and released from sin, is the occasion for a new joy. This joy expresses itself in an exuberance of which laughter is not the only, but is certainly one, expression.

IV

We have dealt thus far with humour as a reaction to the incongruities in the character of self and its neighbors. We have discovered it to be a healthy, but an ultimately unavailing, method of dealing with the evils of human nature. But men face other incongruities than those which human foibles and weaknesses present. Human existence itself is filled with incongruities. Life does not make sense as easily as those philosophers, who think they have charted and comprehended everything in a nice system of rationality, would have us believe. Man's life is really based upon a vast incongruity.

Man is a creature who shares all the weaknesses of the other creatures of the world. Yet he is a sublime creature who holds the ages within his memory and touches the fringes of the eternal in his imagination. When he looks into the world within, he finds depths within depths of mystery which are never completely fathomed. Man is a spirit; and among the qualities of his spirit are the capacity to regard himself and the world; and to speculate on the meaning of the whole. This man is, when he is the observer, the very center of the universe. Yet the same man "brings his years to an end like a tale that is told." This man groweth up like grass in the morning which in the evening is cut down and withereth. The brevity of human existence is the most vivid expression and climax of human weakness.

The incongruity of man's greatness and weakness, of his mortality and immortality, is the source of his temptation to evil. Some men seek to escape from their greatness to their weakness; they try to deny the freedom of their spirit in order to achieve the serenity of nature. Some men seek to escape from their weakness to their greatness. But these simple methods of escape are unavailing. The effort to escape into the weakness of nature leads not to the desired serenity but to sensuality. The effort to escape from weakness to greatness leads not to the security but to the evils of greed and lust for power, or to the opposite evils of a spirituality which denies the creaturely limitations of human existence.

The philosophies of the ages have sought to bridge the chasm between the inner and the outer world, between the world of thought in which man is so great and the world of physical extension in which man is so small and impotent. But philosophy can not bridge the chasm. It can only pretend to do so by reducing one world to the dimensions of the other. Thus naturalists, materialists, mechanists, and all philosophers, who view the world as primarily a system of physical relationships, construct a universe of meaning from which man in the full dimension of spirit can find no home. The idealistic philosophers, on the other hand, construct a world of rational coherence in which mind is the very stuff of order, the very foundation of existence. But their systems do not do justice to the large areas of chaos in the world; and they fail to give an adequate account of man himself, who is something less, as well as something more, than mind.

The sense of humour is, in many respects, a more adequate resource for the incongruities of life than the spirit of philosophy. If we are able to laugh at the curious quirks of fortune in which the system of order and meaning which each life constructs within and around itself is invaded, we at least do not make the mistake of prematurely reducing the irrational to a nice system. Things "happen" to us. We make our plans for a career, and sickness frustrates us. We plan our life, and war reduces all plans to chaos. The storms and furies of the world of nature, which can so easily reduce our private schemes to confusion, do of course have their own laws. They "happen" according to a discernible system of causality. There is no question about the fact that there are systems of order in the world. But it is not so easy to discern a total system of order and meaning which will comprehend the various levels of existence in an orderly whole.

To meet the disappointments and frustrations of life, the irrationalities and contingencies with laughter, is a high form of wisdom. Such laughter does not obscure or defy the dark irrationality. It merely yields to it without too much emotion and friction. A humorous acceptance of fate is really the expression of a high form of self-detachment. If men do not take themselves too seriously, if they have some sense of the precarious nature of the human enterprise, they prove that they are looking at the whole drama of life not merely from the circumscribed point of their own interests but from some further and higher vantage point. One thinks for instance of the profound wisdom which underlies the capacity of laughter in the Negro people. Confronted with the cruelties of slavery, and socially too impotent to throw off the yoke, they learned to make their unpalatable situation more sufferable by laughter. There was of course a deep pathos mixed with the humour, a proof of the fact that laughter had reached its very limit.

There is indeed a limit to laughter in dealing with life's frustrations. We can laugh at all of life's surface irrationalities. We preserve our sanity the more surely if we do not try to reduce the whole crazy-quilt of events in which we move to a premature and illusory order. But the ultimate incongruities of human existence can not be "laughed off." We can not laugh at death. We do try of course.

A war era is particularly fruitful of *Galgenhumor* (gallows humour). Soldiers are known on occasion to engage in hysterical laughter when nerves are tense before the battle. They speak facetiously of the possible dire fate which might befall this or that man of the company. "Sergeant," a soldier is reported to have said before a recent battle, "don't let this little fellow go into battle before me. He isn't big enough to stop the bullet meant for me." The joke was received with uproarious good humour by the assembled comrades. But when the "little fellow" died in battle the next day, everyone felt a little ashamed of the joke. At any rate it was quite inadequate to deal with the depth and breadth of the problem of death.

If we persist in laughter when dealing with the final problem of human existence, when we turn life into a comedy we also reduce it to meaninglessness. That is why laughter, when pressed to solve the ultimate issue, turns into a vehicle of bitterness rather than joy. To laugh at life in the ultimate sense means to scorn it. There is a note of derision in that laughter and an element of despair in that derision.

Just as laughter is the "no-man's land" between cynicism and contrition when we deal with the incongruous element of evil in our own soul, so is it also the area between despair and faith when dealing with evil and incongruity in the world about us. Our provisional amusement with the irrational and unpredictable fortunes which invade the order and purpose of our life must move either toward bitterness or faith, when we consider not this or that frustration and this or that contingent event, but when we are forced to face the issue of the basic incongruity of death.

Either we have a faith from the standpoint of which we are able to say, "I am persuaded, that neither death, nor life . . . shall be able to separate us from the love of God, which is in Christ Jesus our Lord," [1] or we are overwhelmed by the incongruity of death and are forced to say with Ecclesiastes: "I said in mine heart concerning the estate of the sons of men . . . that they might see that they themselves are beasts. For that which befalleth the sons of men befalleth beasts; . . . as the one dieth, so dieth the other; yea they all have one breath; so that a man hath no preeminence above a beast; for all is vanity." [2]

The final problem of human existence is derived from the fact that in one context and from one perspective man has no preeminence above the beast; and yet from another perspective his preeminence is very great. No beast comes to the melancholy conclusion that "all is vanity"; for the purposes of its life do not outrun its power, and death does not therefore invade its life as an irrelevance. Furthermore it has no pre-

[1] Rom. 8:38-39.   [2] Eccles. 3:18-19.

vision of its own end and is therefore not tempted to melancholy. Man's melancholy over the prospect of death is the proof of his partial transcendence over the natural process which ends in death. But this is only a partial transcendence and man's power is not great enough to secure his own immortality.

This problem of man, so perfectly and finally symbolized in the fact of death, can be solved neither by proving that he has no preeminence above the beast, nor yet proving that his preeminence is a guarantee that death has no final dominion over him. Man is both great and small, both strong and weak, both involved in and free of the limits of nature; and he is a unity of strength and weakness of spirit and creatureliness. There is therefore no possibility of man extricating himself by his own power from the predicament of his amphibious state.

The Christian faith declares that the ultimate order and meaning of the world lies in the power and wisdom of God who is both Lord of the whole world of creation and the Father of human spirits. It believes that the incongruities of human existence are finally overcome by the power and the love of God, and that the love which Christ revealed is finally sufficient to overcome the contradiction of death.

This faith is not some vestigial remnant of a credulous and pre-scientific age with which "scientific" generations may dispense. There is no power in any science or philosophy, whether in a pre- or post-scientific age, to leap the chasm of incongruity by pure thought. Thought which begins on one side of the chasm can do no more than deny the reality on the other side. It seeks either to prove that death is no reality because spirit is eternal, or that spirit is not eternal because death is a reality. But the real situation is that man, as a part of the natural world, brings his years to an end like a tale that is told; and that man as a free spirit finds the brevity of his years incongruous and death an irrationality; and that man as a unity of body and spirit can neither by taking thought reduce the dimension of his life to the limit of nature, nor yet raise it to the dimension of pure spirit. Either his incomplete and frustrated life is completed by a power greater than his own, or it is not completed.

Faith is therefore the final triumph over incongruity, the final assertion of the meaningfulness of existence. There is no other triumph and will be none, no matter how much human knowledge is enlarged. Faith is the final assertion of the freedom of the human spirit, but also the final acceptance of the weakness of man and the final solution for the problem of life through the disavowal of any final solutions in the power of man.

Insofar as the sense of humour is a recognition of incongruity, it is more profound than any philosophy which seeks to devour incongruity in reason. But the sense of humour remains healthy only when it deals with immediate issues and faces the obvious and surface irrationalities. It must move toward faith or sink into despair when the ultimate issues are raised.

That is why there is laughter in the vestibule of the temple, the echo of laughter in the temple itself, but only faith and prayer, and no laughter, in the holy of holies.

VIII

THE POWER AND WEAKNESS OF GOD

"And when they had platted a crown of thorns, they put it upon his head, and a reed in his right hand: and they bowed the knee before him, and mocked him, saying, Hail, King of the Jews! And they spit upon him, and took the reed, and smote him on the head. And after that they had mocked him, they took the robe off him, and put his own raiment on him, and led him away to crucify him. . . . And they that passed by reviled him, wagging their heads, And saying, Thou that destroyest the temple, and buildest it in three days, save thyself. If thou be the Son of God, come down from the cross. Likewise also the chief priests mocking him, with the scribes and elders, said, He saved others; himself he cannot save. If he be King of Israel, let him come down from the cross. . . . The thieves also, which were crucified with him, cast the same in his teeth." Mt. 27:29–31, 39–42, 44.

THEY mocked and derided him. The chief priest and scribes, the soldiers and passersby, and even the thieves, were all agreed in regarding the royal and divine pretensions of this Messiah as ridiculous. He was dying upon the cross. Could anything disprove and invalidate the Messianic claim more irrefutably than this ignominious death? He was weak and powerless. He had saved others but could not save himself. If he were any kind of king he ought to have the power to get down from the cross.

All this mockery and derision is the natural and inevitable response to the absurdity of weakness and suffering in a royal and divine figure. Common sense assumes that the most significant and necessary attribute of both royalty and divinity is power. The judgments of priests and soldiers, of passersby, and thieves may vary on other matters. But they are naturally unanimous in their derision of the royal and divine claims of a Messiah upon the cross.

The Christian faith has made this absurdity of a suffering Messiah into the very keystone of its arch of faith. It therefore allows the records to report the derision of the onlookers at Calvary. It feels that the mockery helps to measure the profundity of the revelation upon the cross. If common sense could comprehend this absurdity, that would be proof that there was no depth of revelation in it. A faith which understands the scandal of the cross also has some appreciation of the negative support which mockery gives to the sublimity of the truth apprehended by faith. In the words of a modern literary critic: "The image of Christ crucified is, of all Christian images, the one that in itself contains the full paradox of human doubt and human faith, the focal point of the temporal and the eternal, at which the eternal is at once most essentially challenged and most essentially triumphant." [1]

What is involved in the apprehension of Christian faith that a crucified Christ is the "focal point between the temporal and the eternal," the most luminous symbol of the divine in the historical, the best "handle" by which to grasp the meaning of the divine mystery, is its understanding of the paradox of the power and the weakness of God. The crux of the cross is its revelation of the fact that the final power of God over man is derived from the self-imposed weakness of his love. This self-imposed weakness does not derogate from the Majesty of God. His mercy is the final dimension of His majesty. This is the Christian answer to the final problem of human existence. The worship of God is reverence toward the mysterious source and end of all of life's vitalities; and toward the mysterious source and end of all goodness. A truly "holy" God must be both powerful and good. Impotent or limited goodness is not divine. It can not be worshipped. Its weakness arouses pity rather than worship; and faith is distracted by thought of the power against which this goodness must contend.

[1] Kathleen Raine, "John Donne and Baroque Doubt," *Horizon*, June 1945.

But power without goodness can not be worshipped either. It may be feared, or possibly defied; but reverence must be withheld. Bertrand Russell suggested in his *Free Man's Worship* that the highest religion is for man to "sustain for a moment the world which his own ideals have builded against the trampling march of unconscious power." But such defiance is only one step from despair. If the ultimate source of all of life's vitalities is the evil of "unconscious power," the sense of futility must finally overcome the attitude of noble defiance.

Faith has never been willing to be embarrassed on this issue by the consistencies of the philosophers. Even before the revelation of the cross, the "Holiness" of God has always been conceived as implying both majesty and goodness, both power and love. Yet the two attributes of God stand, at least partly, in contradiction to each other. If God is all-powerful He must be the Creator of evil as well as of good. All the suffering of the world would seem to be finally attributed to Him. If the suffering is due to disharmonies in the order of the world, which God has not mastered, and to recalcitrant forces which He has not subdued, the goodness of God becomes more sharply defined; but His power is called into question. This rational contradiction lies at the heart of faith's apprehension of the Holiness of God. It is never completely resolved. The significance of the revelation in Christ is that the intellectual embarrassment is overcome. The mockery of the absurdity of the weakness of God is cheerfully accepted as a tribute to the truth of the revelation. And all the ages of faith have found in the crucified Lord a luminous point which "makes sense" of the eternal mystery by defying the conclusions of common sense.

II

One reason why the Christian faith is able to resolve the seeming conflict between the idea of the divine power and the divine goodness is that it does not allow that conflict to be absolute. It does not accept the idea that power is of itself evil; and that the source of all power must therefore be lacking in holiness. One of the attributes of holiness is undoubtedly majesty. The Apostles' Creed begins with the credo: "I believe in God the Father Almighty, Maker of heaven and earth." The closing ascription in our Lord's prayer is: "For thine is the power and the glory forever." In a majestic passage in Deutero-Isaiah, God is made to utter the most sweeping claims of power: "I form the light, and create darkness; I make peace, and create evil. I the Lord do all these things." [1]

The power of God is conceived in biblical faith, primarily in twofold terms: It is the power of the Creator of the world and the power of judgment

[1] Isa. 45:7.

which sets a final bound to the evil in the world. The divine power brings forth all the myriad forms of life on the one hand and maintains order and harmony among them on the other. Human history by reason of human freedom had the capacity to defy the order which God has set for His creation; but there are limits to this defiance. He "bringeth the princes to nothing; he maketh the judges of the earth as vanity." [2]

The acceptance of the goodness of power in the Christian faith is intimately related to its whole "non-spiritual" interpretation of life. It never abstracts the spiritual and ideal form from the dynamic stuff of life, to call the one good and the other evil. The created world as such is good; and all forms of creation represent various strategies of power. Life is power; but all created power points beyond itself to an ultimate source. The fact that life is power is not the cause of the evil in it; and the power of the Creator is not a contradiction, but an aspect of His Holiness.

Furthermore, the power of God as judge is holy. God is the ultimate source of that indestructible order in the world against which man's pride and self-will beats in vain. Here the Christian faith, drawing its conceptions of divine justice from the teachings of the Old Testament prophets, reveals similarities with the interpretations of the Greek tragedies, in which the

[2] Isa. 40:23.

power of Zeus is conceived of as the final order and power which ultimately defeats all lesser majesties and forces which are arrayed against it. All lesser sources of power, which seek proudly to usurp the position of Zeus, are finally brought low. Greek tragedy is not quite sure whether the "jealousy" of Zeus is really a source of justice; because it is not certain whether the vitalities and ambitions of the heroes of history, who defy Zeus, may not be noble and heroic and whether the jealousy of Zeus is not an unjustified egotism. There is, in other words, no consistency in dealing with the world as a unity and harmony. Sometimes Zeus is the divine protector of the ultimate harmony and order of the world. And sometimes those who defy him are the necessary heroic protagonists of the various powers and values of the world.

In the Bible, particularly in Hebraic prophetism, there is no question about this point. The nations, judges, and princes of the world are all in partial defiance of the divine creator and judge of the world; and the terrible character of His wrath is a justified judgment upon the various idolatries of history. For all lesser gods are false gods. Only the real God, who is the final source and end of all existence, deserves the unqualified worship which the lesser gods claim for themselves.

We have had ample proof in our own day of the efficacy of power in setting the outer limits of order in the world. We have lived through a great war in which the idolatrous pretensions of a "master race" have been defeated by power. These pretensions clothed themselves in the majesties of power and had to be defeated by power. The human instruments by which the defeat of tyranny was encompassed were of course themselves tainted with some of the evil against which they fought. There are no perfect human instruments of either the divine power or the divine mercy. But we can not escape the responsibilities of power by preoccupation with these corruptions. Life is power. Power is not evil of itself; but evil incarnates itself in power and can not finally be defeated without the use of power. There are always highly "spiritualized" forms of faith which assume that the only hope of virtue among us is to disavow power; and that a virtue which is as impotent as it is good will, by that impotence, achieve the spiritual power to defeat evil. There is an ultimate truth in this contention at which we must look presently. Immediately it is not true. In any immediate situation neither man nor God can defeat a powerful defiance of the order of the world without using power to set the limits of that defiance. There is no purely spiritual method of preserving minimal justice and order in a world; for the world is not purely spiritual. Power is the basis of justice in history as it is of order in the entire natural world. To declare the omnipotence of God is to insist that the ultimate power which maintains the order of the world is superior to all subordinate powers and majesties which tend to create anarchy by making themselves the premature and inadequate centers of order in the world.

III

Yet, despite the certainty of biblical faith that God is all-powerful, it looks upon the crucified Messiah as the final revelation of the divine character and the divine purpose. This divine representative was so powerless that he could not save himself, and he died an ignominious death. One reason why his claims to Messianic authority were rejected by the leaders of the Jews was because they expected a Messiah who would combine perfect power and perfect goodness. That was the meaning of the hope of a "shepherd king" which informed the Messianic expectations not only of Hebraic prophets but of Egyptian and Babylonian prophets before them. Always in human history the same power which maintained order in the world also introduced injustice into the order by reason of the selfish use which the king made of his power. How could history finally culminate in a reign of perfect righteousness except by a divine king who would combine justice with absolute power? This was the expectation. The expectation was doomed to disappointment. Perfect power and goodness can be united only in God, where the contest of life with life is transcended and where the possession of power does not lead to its misuse in the struggle for existence. In human history disinterested power is never as disinterested as it claims to be. It always insinuates something of the special interests of a participant in the struggle of life into the pretended position of disinterested preservation of justice. Thus the so-called democratic nations were good enough to preserve a measure of justice against tyranny in recent conflicts. But the idea, which they have written into the Charter of the United Nations, that there are "peace-loving" nations who can be absolutely distinguished from the peace-breaking ones, obviously does not bear close inspection. The peace of the coming centuries will be less than a perfect or stable peace because Russia, Britain, and America will compound their concern for justice with a concern for their own prestige and power. Every "shepherd king" of history is more king and less shepherd than he pretends. That is as true, in an ultimate sense, of democratic centers of power as of tyrannical ones, though the former are prevented by wisely constructed social checks upon their power from following the logic of selfish power to its final conclusion.

For this reason the revelation of the divine goodness in history must be powerless. The Christ is led as a lamb to the slaughter. He can not save himself from the cross. No human cause or interest gains a triumph through him; all human interests and causes are revealed as practically in contradiction to the divine goodness because "all seek their own." The best law of his day (Roman law) and the best religion of his day (Hebraic monotheism) are implicated in the crucifixion, though the latter expected to be the righteous victor who would gain a triumph over its unrighteous foes in the coming of the Messiah. Christ is thus doubly an offense to the common sense of mankind. He possesses no royal trappings of power and no divine symbols of omnipotence. He is an offense also because he convicts the righteous as well as the unrighteous by his impotent goodness. Therefore the Christian faith regards this scene at the cross as an ultimate point of illumination on the character of man and of God. It was inevitable that this ultimate illumination should be mistaken again and again in human history for proximate forms of moral illumination and thus lead to pacifist illusions. According to such interpretations, the goodness of Christ is a form of powerless goodness which can be emulated by the mere disavowal of power. In such interpretations the tragic culmination of the cross is obscured. It is assumed that powerless goodness achieves the spiritual influence to overcome all forms of evil clothed with other than spiritual forms of power. It is made an instrument of one historical cause in conflict with other historical causes. It becomes the tool of an interested position in society; and a bogus promise of historical success is given to it. Powerless goodness ends upon the cross. It gives no certainty of victory to comparatively righteous causes in conflict with comparatively unrighteous ones. It can only throw a divine illumination upon the whole meaning of history and convict both the righteous and the unrighteous in their struggles. Men may indeed emulate the powerless goodness of Christ; and some of his followers ought indeed to do so. But they ought to know what they are doing. They are not able by this strategy to guarantee a victory for any historical cause, however comparatively virtuous. They can only set up a sign and symbol of the Kingdom of God, of a Kingdom of perfect righteousness and peace which transcends all the struggles of history.

This aspect of the revelatory mission of Christ is expressed in the Christian creeds by the distinction between God the Father and God the Son, between the "Father Almighty, Maker of heaven and earth," and His "only begotten Son" who "was crucified dead and buried." The distinction is between the divine power which underlies all creation and the divine as it appears powerless in history. Most of the efforts to reduce this distinction to nice metaphysical points of discrimination and to indicate just how much of the divine omnipotence or omniscience the historical revealer of God carried with him into history are meaningless or even confusing. The truth which is revealed in Christ must be apprehended in faith. Faith, as far as it uses our natural endowments, draws on poetic and imaginative capacities rather than rational ones. The point of the Christian story is that we see a clue to the character of God in the character and the drama of Christ; and we have some understanding of the fact that the similarity of love between God and Christ is partly revealed by the dissimilarity of power in the historical and trans-historical. The divine goodness is a part of the divine majesty and power; but it can appear in history only in powerless, rather than powerful, terms.

IV

Yet this is not the whole meaning of the powerless Christ, comprehended by faith even while it is rejected by the derision and mockery of priests and soldiers. The Christian faith makes a distinction on the one hand between the Father and the Son, between the God above history and the God in history; and on the other hand declares that the two are one. To declare that the two are one is to insist that the distinction between the historical and the trans-historical, between the facet of the divine which appears in history and the plenitude of the divine which bears all history and creation, must not be made too unqualifiedly.

It must not be made absolutely because the weakness of Christ is not merely the weakness which God's revelation in history makes necessary. It is in part the weakness of God, as He is in His nature. It is the weakness of His love.

The weakness of God's love is not the weakness of goodness striving against the recalcitrance of some "given" stuff of creation. It is the self-imposed weakness of His love. If God has created free spirits who have the capacity to defy Him in their freedom, He has created forms of life so independent that even the power of God, acting merely as power, can not reach the final source of their defiance. The divine power, the very structure of the world, the requirements for mutual living which are made part of the very character of human existence, all these are able to set an ultimate limit to man's defiance of the order of creation. The justice and the "wrath" of God can prevent any human rebellion from developing its defiance to the point of ultimate triumph. The devil, according to Christian myth, is able to defy God but not absolutely. The divine order is supported by the divine power.

But such power does not reach the heart of the rebel. We can, as instruments of the divine justice, set a limit to the defiance of tyranny against the justice of our civilized institutions. The nations which engaged in such defiance have been brought low, and their cities lie in dust and ashes. The imagination of faith is right in discerning this doom as part of the divine justice, however much human instruments of this justice may have obscured and brought confusion into the terrible drama. But this punishment does not reach the heart of Germany or Japan. No punishment can. Justice and wrath have a negatively redemptive effect. They prove to men and nations that there are limits beyond which their rebellion can not go. But punishment may prompt men and nations to despair as well as to repentance. There can indeed be no repentance if love does not shine through the justice. It shines through whenever it becomes apparent that the executor of judgment suffers willingly, as guiltless sufferer, with the guilty victim of punishment. Thus the love of parents shines through the punishment which they may have to mete out to childish recalcitrance. If it does not shine through, childish recalcitrance may harden into adolescent rebellion and mature despair. Because such love seldom shines through the punishment which "righteous" victors exact of the "unrighteous" vanquished, the repentance of vanquished nations is extremely difficult.

The Christian story is that, whatever the inadequacies of forgiveness and love may be in the operations of human justice, men ultimately face divine forgiveness as well as divine wrath. The Christ upon the cross is the point of illumination where the ultimate mercy is apprehended. It is not a mercy which cancels out the divine justice; nor does it prove the divine justice to be merely love. There is a hard and terrible facet to justice which stands in contradiction to love. It is not for that reason evil. Justice is good and punishment is necessary. Yet justice alone does not move men to repentance. The inner core of their rebellion is not touched until they behold the executor of judgment suffering with and for the victim of punishment. This is the meaning of "atonement" as apprehended by faith. It is the final meaning and the final mystery of the relation of God to man. Since it is meaning and not pure mystery, faith must explicate what it means even as we seek to do so in these words. Since it is mystery it can not be fully explicated; which is why all theories of the atonement are less illuminating (and sometimes positively confusing) than the apprehension of the mystery and the meaning by faith. Faith rises above all philosophies and theologies in sensing that the weakness of God is His final power. It is the weakness of love which touches the heart of the offender. The mystery lies in the fact that this mercy is partly the fulfillment and partly the contradiction to the justice which punishes. The fact that justice and mercy are one is symbolically expressed in the idea of the unity of Father and Son. The fact that justice and mercy stand in contradiction is symbolically expressed in the distinction between Father and Son and in the idea that the Son bears the wrath of the Father. In less metaphysical and more historic-symbolic terms the unity of mercy and justice are expressed in the biblical idea that "God so loved the world that he gave his only begotten son." The distinction between justice and mercy is expressed by the idea that the Son bears the sufferings which the wrath of the Father exacts.

The moralists of every age and faith, including the Christian faith, regard these insights as meaningless subleties of theologians or as incredible biblical myths which can impress only the ignorant and credulous. They make these disparaging judgments because they have never plumbed the problem of justice and mercy through to its final depth. Even now they divide into two schools, the hard and the soft school. The hard school would seek to persuade a fallen foe to repentance by the rigor of the punishment of the victors. And the soft school would remit punishment and substitute mercy for judgment. The power which maintains the order of the world is good and not evil; but its virtue does not reach into the secret of the human heart. The justice which checks and punishes evil is also good and not evil; but its force is negative and the persuasive power of repentance and redemption is not in it. Thus the final majesty of God is the majesty of His mercy. It is both the completion and the contradiction of His power. This is the truth apprehended in the cross, which resolves the mystery of the relation of justice to mercy, and gives it meaning.

Naturally the final paradoxes of faith are always in peril of disintegration, inside the Christian community as well as outside. Thus there have been Christian heresies (particularly in the extreme form of Marcionism) which make an absolute distinction

POWER AND WEAKNESS OF GOD

between the God of power who is not good and the God of mercy who is good but not powerful. Some very persuasive forms of the Christian faith drift to the very edge of this heresy. In the first world war the most famous of English chaplains, Studdert-Kennedy, allowed his tragic sense of life to be elaborated into a homiletical theology which resolved the Christian paradox and denied every form of the divine majesty and power except the power of love.

One of his best known poems stated his theology as follows:

> "God, the God I love and worship, reigns in sorrow on the Tree,
> Broken, bleeding, but unconquered, very God of God to me.
> All that showy pomp of splendour, all that sheen of angel wings,
> Was not borrowed from the baubles that surround our earthly kings. . . .
> . . . For Thy glory is the glory of Love's loss,
> And Thou hast no other splendour but the splendour of the Cross.
> For in Christ I see the martyrs and the beauty of their pain,
> And in Him I hear the promise that my dead shall rise again.
> High and lifted up, I see Him on the eternal Calvary,
> And two piercèd hands are stretching east and west o'er land and sea.

On my knees I fall and worship that great Cross
  that shines above,
For the very God of Heaven is not Power, but
  Power of Love." [1]

A non-Christian interpretation of the problem of suffering, also presented during the first world war, in H. G. Wells' *God, the Invisible King,* arrived at somewhat the same picture of a kind but not very powerful divine ruler who suffered with man in fighting against the recalcitrance of something in the universe more powerful than himself. Recently some Christian philosophers have sought to present the same doctrine in Christian form.

But all these efforts, however small or great their ingredients of Scriptural content, manage to obscure the sublimity of the paradox which the revelation of God in Christ contains. They are provisionally plausible because they are philosophically more consistent than the Christian doctrine. But they are not true to all of the facts of existence and they fail to illumine the final mystery of justice and mercy, of power and goodness, which is revealed from the cross. Faith, by a wisdom which touches sublimities beyond the ken of philosophies, will thus continue to cherish the scandal of the cross and accept the mockery and derision of the various crowd at Calvary as a kind of tribute to the truth which transcends and fulfills the highest

[1] From "High and Lifted Up" in *The Sorrows of God, And Other Poems,* by G. A. Studdert-Kennedy.

insights of reason. The words of derision: "He saved others, himself he cannot save," gives us a clue to the innermost character of a man in history who perished upon the cross. It also gives us a clue to the mystery of the very character of God.

IX

MYSTERY AND MEANING

"For now we see through a glass darkly; but then face to face: now I know in part; but then shall I know even as also I am known." I Cor. 13:12.

THE testimonies of religious faith are confused more greatly by those who claim to know too much about the mystery of life than by those who claim to know too little. Those who disavow all knowledge of the final mystery of life are so impressed by the fact that we see through a glass darkly that they would make no claim of seeing at all. In the history of culture such a position is known as agnosticism. Agnosticism sees no practical value in seeking to solve the mystery of life. But there are not really many agnostics in any age or culture. A much larger number of people forget that they see through a glass darkly. They claim to know too much.

Those who claim to know too much may be divided into two groups, one ostensibly religious and the other irreligious. The irreligious resolve the problem of human existence and the mystery of the created world into systems of easily ascertained meaning. They deny that there is any mystery in life or the world. If they can find a previous cause for any subsequent effect in nature, they are certain that they have arrived at a full understanding of why such and such a thing exists. The natural cause is, for them, an adequate explanation of anything they may perceive.

The religious group on the other hand recognizes that the whole of the created world is not self-explanatory. They see that it points beyond itself to a mysterious ground of existence, to an enigmatic power beyond all discernible vitalities, and to a "first cause" beyond all known causes. But they usually claim to know too much about this eternal mystery. Sometimes they sharply define the limits of reason, and the further limits of faith beyond reason, and claim to know exactly how far reason penetrates into the eternal mystery, and how much further faith reaches. Yet though they make a distinction between faith and reason, they straightway so mix and confuse reason and faith that they pretend to be able to give a rational and sharply defined account of the character of God and of the eternal ground of existence. They define the power and knowledge of God precisely, and explain the exact extent of His control and foreknowledge of the course of events. They dissect the mysterious relation between man's intellectual faculties and his vital capacities, and claim to know the exact limits of *physis,* *psyche* and *nous,* of body, soul and spirit. They know that man is immortal and why; and just what portion and part of him is mortal and what part immortal. Thus they banish the mystery of the unity of man's spiritual and physical existence. They have no sense of mystery about the problem of immortality. They know the geography of heaven and of hell, and the furniture of the one and the temperature of the other.

A genuine Christian faith must move between those who claim to know so much about the natural world that it ceases to point to any mystery beyond itself and those who claim to know so much about the mystery of the "unseen" world that all reverence for its secret and hidden character is dissipated. A genuine faith must recognize the fact that it is through a dark glass that we see; though by faith we do penetrate sufficiently to the heart of the mystery not to be overwhelmed by it. A genuine faith resolves the mystery of life by the mystery of God. It recognizes that no aspect of life or existence explains itself, even after all known causes and consequences have been traced. All known existence points beyond itself. To realize that it points beyond itself to God is to assert that the mystery of life does not dissolve life into meaninglessness. Faith in God is faith in some ultimate unity of life, in some final comprehensive purpose which holds all the various, and frequently contradictory, realms of coherence and meaning together. A genuine faith does not mark this mysterious source and end of existence as merely an X, or as an unknown quantity. The Christian faith, at least, is a faith in revelation. It believes that God has made Himself known. It believes that He has spoken through the prophets and finally in His Son. It accepts the revelation in Christ as the ultimate clue to the mystery of God's nature and purpose in the world, particularly the mystery of the relation of His justice to His mercy. But these clues to the mystery do not eliminate the periphery of mystery. God remains *deus absconditus*.

Of the prophets of the Old Testament, the Second Isaiah is particularly conscious of the penumbra of mystery which surrounds the eternal and the divine. He insists upon the distance between the divine wisdom and human counsels: "Who hath directed the spirit of the Lord, or being his counsellor hath taught him?"[1] He emphasizes the transcendence of God's power: "It is he that sitteth upon the circle of the earth, and the inhabitants thereof are as grasshoppers ... that bringeth the princes to nothing; he maketh the judges of the earth as vanity."[2] The question of the meaning of life must not be pressed too far, according to the prophet: "Woe unto him that striveth with his Maker.... Shall the clay say to him that fashioneth it, What makest thou? ... Woe unto him that saith unto his father, What begettest thou? or to the woman, What hast thou brought forth?"[3]

[1] Isa. 40:13.   [2] Isa. 40:22-23.   [3] Isa. 45:9-10.

Faith, as the prophet conceives it, discerns the meaning of existence but must not seek to define it too carefully. The divine wisdom and purpose must always be partly hid from human understanding—"For my thoughts are not your thoughts, neither are your ways my ways, saith the Lord. For as the heavens are higher than the earth, so are my ways higher than your ways, and my thoughts than your thoughts." [4]

The sense of both mystery and meaning is perhaps most succinctly expressed in the forty-fifth chapter of Isaiah, where, practically in the same breath, the prophet declares on the one hand, "Verily thou art a God that hidest thyself, O God of Israel, the Saviour," [5] and on the other, insists that God has made Himself known: "I have not spoken in secret, in a dark place of the earth: I said not unto the seed of Jacob, Seek ye me in vain: I the Lord speak righteousness, I declare things that are right." [6] This double emphasis is a perfect symbolic expression both of the meaning which faith discerns and of the penumbra of mystery which it recognizes around the core of meaning. The essential character of God, in His relations to the world, is known. He is the Creator, Judge and Saviour of men. Yet He does not fully disclose Himself, and His thoughts are too high to be comprehended by human thought.

[4] Isa. 55:8-9.   [5] Isa. 45:15.   [6] Isa. 45:19.

II

For some centuries the intellectual life of modern man has been dominated by rebellion against medieval faith. The main outlines of modern culture are defined by modern man's faith in science and his defiance of the authority of religion. This conflict between the faith which flowered in the thirteenth century and that which flowered in the seventeenth and eighteenth centuries is a conflict between two forms of faith which in their different ways obscured the penumbra of the mystery of life and made the core of meaning too large. Medieval Catholicism was not completely lacking in a reverent sense of mystery. The rites of the Church frequently excel the more rationalized forms of the Protestant faith by their poetic expression of mystery. There is, for instance, an advantage in chanting rather than saying a creed. The musical and poetical forms of a creed emphasize the salient affirmation of faith which the creed contains, and slightly derogate the exact details of symbolism through which the basic affirmation is expressed. That is a virtue of the liturgical and sacramental Church, which is hardened into a pitiless fundamentalism when every "i" is dotted and every "t" crossed in the soberly recited credo.

On the other hand the same Catholic faith combined a pretentious rationalism with its sense of poetry. Any careful reading of the works of Thomas Aquinas must impress the thoughtful student with the element of pretension which informs the flowering of the Catholic faith in the "golden" thirteenth century. There seems to be no mystery which is not carefully dissected, and no dark depth of evil which is not fully explained, and no height of existence which is not scaled. The various attributes of God are all carefully defined and related to each other. The mysteries of the human soul and spirit are mastered and rationally defined in the most meticulous terms. The exact line which marks justice from injustice is known. Faith and reason are so intermingled that the characteristic certainty of each is compounded with the other. Thus a very imposing structure is created. Yet it ought to have been possible to anticipate the doubts which it would ultimately arouse. Granted its foundation of presuppositions, every beam and joist in the intellectual structure is reared with perfect logical consistency. But the foundation is insecure. It is a foundation of faith in which the timeless affirmations of the Christian belief are compounded with detailed knowledge characteristic of a pre-scientific age. An age of science challenged this whole foundation of presupposition and seemed to invalidate the whole structure.

The new age of science attempted an even more rigorous denial of mystery. The age of science traced the relations of the world of nature, studied the various causes which seemed to be at the root of various effects in every realm of natural coherence; and came to the conclusion that knowledge dissolved mystery. Mystery was simply the darkness of ignorance which the light of knowledge dispelled. Religious faith was, in its opinion, merely the fear of the unknown which could be dissipated by further knowledge. In the one case the "spiritual," the "eternal" and the "supernatural," conceived as a separate and distinct realm of existence (instead of as the final ground and ultimate dimension of the unity of existence), is so exactly defined that the penumbra of mystery is destroyed. In the other case the "natural," the "temporal" and the "material" are supposedly comprehended so fully that they cease to point beyond themselves to a more ultimate mystery. There are significant differences between these two ways of apprehending the world about us and the depth of existence within us; but the differences are no greater than the similarity between them. Both ways contain an element of human pretension. Both fail to recognize that we see through a glass darkly.

III

We see through a glass darkly when we seek to understand the world about us; because no natural cause is ever a complete and adequate explanation of the subsequent event. The subsequent event is undoubtedly causally related to preceding events; but it is only one of many untold possibilities which might have been actualized. The biblical idea of a divine creator moves on a different level than scientific concepts of causation. The two become mutually exclusive, as they have done in the controversies of recent ages, only if, on the one hand, we deny the mysterious element in creation and regard it as an exact explanation of why things are as they are and become what they become; and if, on the other hand, we deny the mystery which overarches the process of causation in nature. Thus two dimensions of meaning, each too exactly defined, come in conflict with each other. More truly and justly conceived, the realm of coherence, which we call nature, points to a realm of power beyond itself. This realm is discerned by faith, but not fully known. It is a mystery which resolves the mystery of nature. But if mystery is denied in each realm, the meaning which men pretend to apprehend in each becomes too pat and calculated. The depth of meaning is destroyed in the process of charting it exactly. Thus the sense of meaning is deepened, and not annulled, by the sense of mystery.

The understanding of ourselves is even more subject to seeing through a glass darkly than the understanding of the world about us. We "are fearfully and wonderfully made." Man is a creature of nature, subject to its necessities and bound by its limits. Yet he surveys the ages and touches the fringes of the eternal. Despite the limited character of his life, he is constantly under compulsions and responsibilities which reach to the very heart of the eternal.

> "Thou hast beset me behind and before,
> And laid thine hand upon me.
> Such knowledge is too wonderful for me;
> It is high, I cannot attain unto it."

confesses the Psalmist in recording the universal human experience of feeling related to a divine lawgiver and judge.

> "Whither shall I go from thy spirit?
> Or whither shall I flee from thy presence?
> If I ascend into heaven, thou art there:
> If I make my bed in hell, behold, thou art there.
> If I take the wings of the morning,
> And dwell in the uttermost parts of the sea;
> Even there shall thy hand lead me,
> And thy right hand shall hold me."[1]

Thus the Psalmist continues in describing the boundless character of the human spirit, which rises above and beyond all finite limitations to confront and feel itself confronted by the divine.

The finiteness of human life, contrasted with the limitless quality of the human spirit, presents us with a profound mystery. We are an enigma to ourselves.

There are many forms of modern thought which deny the mystery of our life by reducing the dimen-

[1] Psalm 139.

sion of human existence to the level of nature. We are animals, we are told, with a slightly greater reach of reason and a slightly "more complex central nervous system" than the other brute creatures. But this is a palpable denial of the real stature of man's spirit. We may be only slightly more inventive than the most astute monkey. But there is, as far as we know, no *Weltschmerz* in the soul of any monkey, no anxiety about what he is and ought to be, and no visitation from a divine accuser who "besets him behind and before" and from whose spirit he can not flee. There is among animals no uneasy conscience and no ambition which tends to transgress all natural bounds and become the source of the highest nobility of spirit and of the most demonic madness.

We are a mystery to ourselves in our weakness and our greatness; and this mystery can be resolved in part only as we reach into the height of the mysterious dimension of the eternal into which the pinnacle of our spiritual freedom seems to rise. The mystery of God resolves the mystery of the self into meaning. By faith we find the source of our life: "It is he that hath made us and not we ourselves." Here too we find the author of our moral duties: "He that judgeth me is the Lord." And here is the certitude of our fulfillment: "But then shall I know even as also I am known," declares St. Paul. This is to say that despite the height of our vision no man can complete the structure of meaning in which he is involved except as by faith he discerns that he "is known," though he himself only "knows in part." The human spirit reaches beyond the limit of nature and does not fully comprehend the level of reality into which it reaches. Any interpretation of life which denies this height of reality because it ends in mystery gives a false picture of the stature of man. On the other hand any interpretation which seeks to comprehend the ultimate dimension by the knowledge and the symbols of the known world also gives a false picture of man. Such theologies obscure the finiteness of human knowledge. We see through a glass darkly when we seek to discern the divine ground and end of human experience; we see only by faith. But by faith we do see.

IV

The source of the evil in us is almost as mysterious as the divine source and the end of our spiritual life. "O Lord," cried the prophet, "why hast thou made us to err from thy ways, and hardened our heart from thy fear?"[1] We desire the good and yet do evil. In the words of St. Paul, "I delight in the law of God after the inward man: but I see another law in my members, warring against the law of my mind."[2] The inclination to evil, which is primarily the inclination to inordinate self-love, runs counter to our conscious

[1] Isa. 63:17.   [2] Rom. 7:22-23.

desires. We seem to be betrayed into it. "Now if I do that I would not, it is no more I that do it, but sin that dwelleth in me," [3] declares St. Paul, in trying to explain the powerful drift toward evil in us against our conscious purposes. There is a deep mystery here which has been simply resolved in modern culture. It has interpreted man as an essentially virtuous creature who is betrayed into evil by ignorance, or by evil economic, political, or religious institutions. These simple theories of historical evil do not explain how virtuous men of another generation created the evil in these inherited institutions, or how mere ignorance could give the evil in man the positive thrust and demonic energy in which it frequently expresses itself. Modern culture's understanding of the evil in man fails to do justice to the tragic and perplexing aspect of the problem.

Orthodox Christianity on the other hand has frequently given a dogmatic answer to the problem, which suggests mystery, but which immediately obscures the mystery by a dogmatic formula. Men are evil, Christian orthodoxy declared, because of the "sin of Adam" which has been transmitted to all men. Sometimes the mode of transmission is allowed to remain mysterious; but sometimes it is identified with the concupiscence in the act of procreation. This dogmatic explanation has prompted the justified protest and incredulity of modern man, particularly since it

[3] Rom. 7:20.

is generally couched in language and symbols taken from a pre-scientific age.

Actually there is a great mystery in the fact that man, who is so created that he can not fulfill his life except in his fellowmen, and who has some consciousness of this law of love in his very nature, should nevertheless seek so persistently to make his fellowmen the tools of his desires and the objects of his ambitions. If we try to explain this tendency toward self-love, we can find various plausible explanations. We can say it is due to the fact that man exists at the juncture of nature and spirit, of freedom and necessity. Being a weak creature, he is anxious for his life; and being a resourceful creature, armed with the guile of spirit, he seeks to overcome his insecurity by the various instruments which are placed at his disposal by the resources of his freedom. But inevitably the security which he seeks for himself is bought at the price of other men's security. Being an insignificant creature with suggestions of great significance in the stature of his freedom, man uses his strength to hide his weakness and thus falls into the evil of the lust for power and self-idolatry.

These explanations of man's self-love are plausible enough as far as they go. But they are wrong if they assume that the peculiar amphibious situation of man, being partly immersed in the time process and partly transcending it, must inevitably and necessarily tempt him to an inordinate self-love. The situation does not create evil if it is not falsely interpreted. From whence comes the false interpretation? There is thus great profundity in the biblical myth of the serpent who "tempted" Eve by suggesting that God was jealous of man's strength and sought to limit it. Man's situation tempts to evil, provided man is unwilling to accept the peculiar weakness of his creaturely life, and is unable to find the ultimate source and end of his existence beyond himself. It is man's unbelief and pride which tempt to sin. And every such temptation presupposes a previous "tempter" (of which the serpent is the symbol). Thus before man fell into sin there was, according to Biblical myth, a fall of the devil in heaven. The devil is a fallen angel who refused to accept his rightful place in the scheme of things and sought a position equal to God.

This then is the real mystery of evil; that it presupposes itself. No matter how far back it is traced in the individual or the race, or even preceding the history of the race, a profound scrutiny of the nature of evil reveals that there is an element of sin in the temptation which leads to sin; and that, without this presupposed evil, the consequent sin would not necessarily arise from the situation in which man finds himself. This is what Kierkegaard means by saying that "sin posits itself." This is the mystery of "original sin" about which Pascal truly observes that "without this mystery man remains a mystery to himself."

Purely sociological and historical explanations of

the rise of evil do not touch the depth of the mystery at all. Christian dogmatic explanations have some sense of it; but they obscure it as soon as they have revealed it by their pat dogmatic formulae. In dealing with the problem of sin the sense of meaning is inextricably interwoven with the sense of mystery. We see through a glass darkly when we seek to understand the cause and the nature of evil in our own souls. But we see more profoundly when we know it is through a dark glass that we see than if we pretend to have clear light upon this profound problem.

V

The final mystery about human life concerns its incompleteness and the method of its completion. Here again modern culture has resolved all mystery into simple meaning. It believes that the historical process is such that it guarantees the ultimate fulfillment of all legitimate human desires. It believes that history, as such, is redemptive. Men may be frustrated today, may live in poverty and in conflict, and may feel that they "bring their years to an end like a tale that is told." But the modern man is certain that there will be a tomorrow in which poverty and war and all injustice will be abolished. Utopia is the simple answer which modern culture offers in various guises to the problem of man's ultimate frustration.

History is, according to the most characteristic thought of modern life, a process which gradually closes the hiatus between what man is and what he would be. The difficulty with this answer is that there is no evidence that history has any such effect. In the collective enterprises of man, the progress of history arms the evil, as well as the good, with greater potency; and the mystery of how history is to be brought to completion, therefore, remains on every level of human achievement. It may in fact express itself more poignantly in the future than in the past.

Furthermore, there is no resolution of the problem of the individual in any collective achievement of mankind. The individual must continue to find the collective life of man his ultimate moral frustration, as well as his fulfillment. For there is no human society, and there can be none, the moral mediocrity of which must not be shocking to the individual's highest moral scruples. Furthermore, the individual dies before any of the promised collective completions of history.

But this is not all. The problem of death is deeply involved with the problem of sin. Men die with an uneasy conscience and must confess with the Psalmist, "for we are consumed by thine anger and by thy wrath are we troubled." Any honest self-analysis must persuade us that we end our life in frustration not only because "our reach is beyond our grasp," i.e., because we are finite creatures with more than finite conceptions of an ultimate consummation of life, but also because we are sinners who constantly introduce positive evil into the operations of divine providence.

The answer of Christian faith to this problem is belief in "the forgiveness of sin and life everlasting." We believe that only a power greater than our own can complete our incomplete life, and only a divine mercy can heal us of our evil. Significantly St. Paul adds this expression of Christian hope immediately to his confession that we see through a glass darkly. We see through a glass darkly now, "but then" we shall "see face to face." Now we "know in part" but "then" we shall know even as we are known. This Christian hope makes it possible to look at all the perplexities and mysteries of life without too much fear.

In another context St. Paul declares: "We are perplexed, but not unto despair." One might well divide the world into those who are not perplexed, those who are perplexed unto despair, and those who are perplexed but not unto despair. Those who are not perplexed have dissolved all the mysteries and perplexities of life by some simple scheme of meaning. The scheme is always too simple to do justice to the depth of man's problem. When life reveals itself in its full terror, as well as its full beauty, these little schemes break down. Optimism gives way to despair. The Christian faith does not pretend to resolve all perplexities. It confesses the darkness of human sight and the perplexities of faith. It escapes despair nevertheless because it holds fast to the essential goodness of God as revealed in Christ, and is therefore "persuaded that neither life nor death—are able to separate us from the love of God, which is in Christ Jesus our Lord."

It can not be denied, however, that this same Christian faith is frequently vulgarized and cheapened to the point where all mystery is banished. The Christian faith in heaven is sometimes as cheap as, and sometimes even more vulgar than, the modern faith in Utopia. It may be even less capable of expressing the final perplexity and the final certainty of faith. On this issue, as on the others we have considered, a faith which measures the final dimension of existence, but dissipates all mystery in that dimension, may be only a little better or worse than a shallow creed which reduces human existence to the level of nature.

Our situation is that, by reason of the freedom of our spirit, we have purposes and ends beyond the limits of the finiteness of our physical existence. Faith may discern the certainty of a final completion of life beyond our power, and a final purging of the evil which we introduce into life by our false efforts to complete it in our own strength. But faith can not resolve the mystery of how this will be done. When we look into the future we see through a glass darkly. The important issue is whether we will be tempted by the incompleteness and frustration of life to despair; or whether we can, by faith, lay hold on the divine power and wisdom which completes what remains otherwise incomplete. A faith which resolves mystery too much denies the finiteness of all human knowledge, including the knowledge of faith. A faith which is overwhelmed by mystery denies the clues of divine meaning which shine through the perplexities of life. The proper combination of humility and trust is precisely defined when we affirm that we see, but admit that we see through a glass darkly.

VI

Our primary concern in this exposition of the Pauline text has been to understand the fact that the Christian faith is conscious of the penumbra of mystery which surrounds its conception of meaning. Yet in conclusion it must be emphasized that our faith can not be identified with poetic forms of religion which worship mystery without any conception of meaning. All such poetic forms of faith might well be placed in the category of the worship of the unknown God, typified in the religion which Paul found in Athens. In contrast to this religion Paul set the faith which is rooted in the certainty that the mysterious God has made Himself known, and that the revelation of His nature and purpose, apprehended by faith, must be declared: "Whom therefore ye ignorantly worship him declare I unto you." This declaration of faith rests upon the belief that the divine is not mere mystery, the heart of it having been disclosed to those who are able to apprehend the divine disclosure in Christ. It is by the certainty of that faith that St. Paul can confidently look toward a future completion of our imperfect knowledge: "Now I know in part, but *then* shall I know." The indication that faith regards the meaning, which has been disclosed, as victorious over the mystery of existence is the expression of a certain hope that "then shall I know." Faith expects that ultimately all mystery will be resolved in the perfect knowledge of God.

Faith in a religion of revelation is thus distinguished on the one side from merely poetic appreciations of mystery, just as on the other side it is distinguished from philosophies of religion which find the idea of revelation meaningless. Revelation is meaningless to all forms of rational religion which approach the mystery of life with the certainty that human reason can at length entirely resolve the mystery. The Christian faith is the right expression of the greatness and the weakness of man in relation to the mystery and the meaning of life. It is an acknowledgment of human weakness, for, unlike "natural religion" and "natural theology," it does not regard the human mind as capable of resolving the enigma of existence because it knows that human reason is itself involved in the enigma which it tries to comprehend. It is an acknowledgment of the greatness of the human spirit because it assumes that man is capable of apprehending clues to the divine mystery and accepting the disclosure of the purposes of God which He has made to us. It is a confession at once of both weakness and strength, because it recognizes that the disclosures of the divine are given to man, who is capable of apprehending them, when made, but is not capable of anticipating them.

According to the Christian faith there is a light which shineth in darkness; and the darkness is not able to comprehend it. Reason does not light that light; but faith is able to pierce the darkness and apprehend it.

X

THE PEACE OF GOD

"The peace of God, which passeth all understanding, shall keep your hearts and minds through Christ Jesus." Phil. 4:7.

MAN lives in tumult and anxiety, seeking for peace. The greatness and freedom of the human spirit places his life beyond the dimension of nature and makes her peace an impossible security for him. The creatures of nature have an internal peace because they are what they are. They do not have to worry about becoming their true selves. Since all desires and hungers of brute creatures have a natural limit, the frictions and conflicts of the world of nature also move within definite bounds. Nature may be red in tooth and claw; and life may feed on life. But the conflicts of nature do not exceed the bounds which are set in nature's economy.

Man, on the other hand, has no natural peace either within or without. "Within are tumults and without are fears." The tumults within spring from human freedom. None of the impulses which regulate the

THE PEACE OF GOD

functions of animal existence operate in man without the intervention of his thought. They can be extended or repressed. They can not be organized into a living unity without the introduction of a unifying principle and center. What is that center to be? If man makes his life its own center, he destroys himself; for his imagination reaches too far and his capacities are too great for self-sufficiency. But if the center of his life is to be beyond himself, where is that center to be? Man's anxieties and inner fears are prompted both by the abortive effort to center his life within himself and by the uneasiness of trying to find the true center beyond himself.

The fact that there are no natural limits to human desires and ambitions makes man's relation to his fellowmen uneasy and full of discord. Man can not live without the support of his fellowmen; and he can not live truly without offering them his support. But this mutual relation is constantly disturbed by the inordinate claims which the self makes on the community. The social peace of the community is thus an achievement of only the wisest statecraft which knows how to place social checks upon inordinate desires, and which is able to find the best available instruments for encouraging mutual tasks and discouraging predatory and inordinate desires. But even the wisest statecraft can not achieve the harmony within the human community which ants and bees possess by virtue of the instinctive direction of their mutual tasks.

Man's unquiet and restless life is thus the fruit of his special freedom; and of the inevitable corruptions of that freedom by inordinate desire. But he can not accept this anxiety and friction as normal. All creatures, including man, must have peace. Harmony is the normal condition of all existence. All vitalities and centers of life in the whole creation were meant to exist in conformity with their own proper nature and in accord with all other creatures. For this reason man seeks after peace just as certainly as he also seeks after many ends incompatible with it. But what kind of peace is possible for man? How is he to find a peace which will not destroy his essential freedom? Which will not rob him of the unique dignity that distinguishes him from the brute creation?

When we survey this fundamental human problem and explore its full dimension we come upon a perplexing fact. We discover that every form of peace which is easily understood is not adequate for man. Only a peace "which passeth all understanding" is adequate.

There are two forms of peace within the limits of understanding. The one is the peace of nature which leaves human freedom out of consideration; the other is the peace of human reason which is achieved by denying or obscuring the hopes, fears and ambitions, transcending reason, and the impulses and desires, lying below it. Both are simple forms of peace. Both are too simple. The peace of God, on the other hand, is not simple. There is pain and sorrow in it. That at least is the peace of God which has been revealed in the cross of Christ. It passeth understanding to such a degree that the very revelation of it has been an offense to the wise. The wise men of the world have always pictured God as dwelling in a supernal serenity, in an Olympian equanimity, untouched by the sorrows of the world and undisturbed by its tumults. The God who is revealed in Christ is not so easily understood. There is indeed peace in Him and with Him. He is the calm source from which all life springs and the serene end in which all life finds its fulfillment. But strangely and paradoxically there is also sorrow and suffering in His heart; and it is by that sorrow and suffering that He finally overcomes the world's disquiet.

This kind of peace is both difficult to understand and impossible to acquire by striving. That is why men would rather seek for the peace which is within the limits of understanding. Only, unfortunately, they are destroyed by that kind of peace.

II

Though the peace of nature is obviously a Paradise from which man has been expelled and which an angel with a flaming sword guards against his re-entry, history is filled with abortive efforts to return to that peace. In classical antiquity Democritus and

Epicurus, Lucretius and Diogenes and many other wise men, sought to beguile men from their inordinate ambitions by seeking to persuade them to return to nature and live within the limits of desire set by it. In the modern day the same abortive effort has been made, by the German romantics and the French naturalists, by Thoreau and Walt Whitman. The accents of the philosophy of romanticism have varied; but the general strategy is identical. The idea is that there is a peace of nature which man can claim as his own and be redeemed by it.

These philosophies have a certain plausibility because there is a provisionally therapeutic power in the peace of nature. Close communion with nature does quiet many a fear and tumult and exorcise many a devil of care. The poets of every age have discerned this power of nature:

> "The little cares that fretted me,
> I lost them yesterday,
> Among the fields above the sea,
> Among the winds at play,
> Among the lowing of the herds,
> The rustling of the trees,
> Among the singing of the birds,
> The humming of the bees." [1]

The peace of nature is provisionally therapeutic because the majesties and immensities of nature serve

---

[1] Anonymous.

to make the hopes and fears of the human heart slightly ridiculous, thus prompting man to shame for his pretensions. Furthermore the symphony of nature's various quiet melodies—the swish of the grass, the singing of the birds, the lap of the water on the shore, the rustle of the leaves—has a quieting effect upon the human spirit. They are sacramental reminders of the ultimate peace which life must achieve. Within limits, they are even the means of grace for achieving such peace.

But these ministries of nature are only tentative and provisional. Walt Whitman may glory in the animals who are so "peaceful and self-contained" and who "do not lie awake at nights fretting about their sins." But only a little reflection must make it apparent that bovine serenity would annihilate man, were he able to achieve it. The animal may be peaceful because it is self-contained; but man is man precisely because he is not self-contained. His imagination sweeps the heavens and the ages; and all his capacities and needs are so intimately related to those of his fellows that self-sufficiency is an impossible source of equanimity for him. The peace of nature is the fruit of blindness which does not see beyond its little orbit; and of deafness that does not hear a cry of joy or pain beyond its little circle; and of satisfied hungers because they have definite limits. What is man to do with that kind of peace, since his eyes look beyond all horizons and fill him with forebodings of the meaning of the reality beyond; and since his ears are sensitive to all the noises of battle and all the pæans of victory all over the world; and since his spirit gives every hunger of the body an infinite dimension and every craving of the spirit a limitless scope?

The peace of nature may persuade man of the desirability of serenity; and it may even give him a foretaste of it. But it can not really quiet the human heart without destroying man's essential being. How can nature, which does not know what god it serves, help man, who is searching for God and is disquiet because he does not know whether he has found the real God, the true source and end of his existence; or is anxious because he is darkly conscious of the fact that his preoccupation with self is an idolatrous form of worship, placing him under the judgment of the true God?

III

Another form of peace also within the limits of human understanding is supposed to be superior to the peace of nature. It is the peace of a quiet mind. The human mind is of course intimately and organically related to the whole realm of human vitality. Human reason gives our animal purposes a wider, and sometimes a nobler, scope. Our rational faculties may also, as Aristotle observed, bring a certain order into the whole field of our vital impulses and organize and restrain them according to the principle "in nothing too much." A certain degree of both inner and social peace can be achieved by the law of moderation. A prudent restraint upon every ambition and a cautious check upon every desire can serve to create a modicum of harmony within the self; and the check upon inordinate desire can serve to maintain peace with our fellowmen.

But reason itself has no sure criterion of harmony beyond the canon of moderation. It can not determine the supreme loyalty of life. It can not organize life in the proper hierarchy of values. Even if it possessed the criteria to do so, it would not have the final power to moderate the passions. It might produce some cool and calculating discipline of life; but such a life would be as devoid of great heroic passion as of destructive mania.

Whenever philosophers become aware of the impotence of reason in its relation to power, desire and ambition, they tend to translate the ideal of a rational peace to a peace of detachment. Thus the Stoics regarded the final and supreme good a form of equanimity (*Ataraxia*) in which the self is completely detached from all of its responsibilities, loyalties and affections, as well as from its hopes, fears and ambitions. This peace of mind is, in other words, not the peace of a real self, but of a mind detached from the self. Insofar as it is achieved the real self is destroyed. It is significant that both Stoicism and Platonism tended to develop this logic of detachment to a consistent mysticism in their latter forms. The final culmination of the process of detachment is a mysticism, in which the self seeks for the peace of an undifferentiated eternity and unity of being. This kind of peace is sometimes defined as "spiritual." If spirit is equated with reason this may be a correct definition. But if man's spirit is the synthesis of his vitality and his reason, the peace of detachment is not spiritual but ends in the destruction of the self as spirit.

A purely rational peace is, in short, as destructive of the whole of man as the pure peace of nature. The peace of nature destroys the whole superstructure of human freedom. The peace of mind destroys man as a unity of body and mind, of vitality and freedom, of instinct and reason.

IV

There are religions which interpret the peace of God as the detached calm and passionless equanimity after which the Stoics and the mystics strive. There are indeed forms of the Christian faith which fail to understand that the peace of God which is revealed in the cross of Christ can not be equated with the peace of detachment. The God of the Bible is both Creator and Redeemer. As Creator He is power as well as wisdom; as Redeemer He is merciful as well as holy. God does not therefore have a simple peace which

THE PEACE OF GOD

the mind can easily comprehend. Creativity involves disturbance and upheaval. To take the "things that are not and put to naught the things that are" means revolutionary activity. To suffer with sinners means pain.

Christian orthodoxy has been rightly afraid of a too consistent emphasis upon the suffering of God. It has declared the doctrine, that God the Father suffers, to be a heresy (the heresy of "patripassionism"). Yet it has affirmed that God the Son suffers and that the Son and the Father are One. To insist on the distinction between the Majesty of the Father and the suffering of the Son, and yet to declare that the Father and the Son are one, is an effort to state, within the limits of human understanding, our comprehension and our lack of comprehension of a form of peace which passeth understanding. If the suffering of God is emphasized too completely we arrive at the heretical conception of a finite God who is frustrated by the inertia of some "given" stuff of reality. If the peace of God is defined too rationally, on the other hand, we arrive at a conception of a peace which is purchased at the price of detachment. To say that there is a final peace in the divine majesty and yet that the pinnacle of that majesty is a mercy which is involved in the sins and sorrows of the world is to speak beyond understanding; but not beyond the apprehension of faith; for faith rightly discerns the Father of the suffering Christ as the real source and end of all human striving; and knows His peace to be the one form of serenity which does not destroy but which fulfills man in the completeness and the unity of his being.

The peace of God is a peace of love. There is no simple peace in love. One need only to compare the ideals of Epictetus with the temper of the New Testament to recognize that perfect detachment and perfect love are incompatible. The peace of love is the most perfect peace, because in it spirit is related to all of life. Yet it is a very imperfect peace because attachment to the pains and sorrows of others subject us, and even God, to those sorrows. That so imperfect a peace should also be the most perfect peace passes understanding. Yet it is the peace of God; and it is also the only possible peace for man.

St. Paul, in the words of our text, expresses the hope that this kind of peace may guard the hearts and minds of Christian people. What does such a benediction imply? How would our hearts be "kept" or "guarded" by such a peace?

The "peace of God" for man is partly achieved by the emulation of God's love. Man is not so created that he can live his life in either calm detachment or cautious self-possession and moderation. He lives most truly according to his nature if his imagination, his sympathies, and his responsibilities draw him out of himself into the life of the community, into the needs, the hopes and aspirations of his fellows. But this self-realization through love is not something which can be achieved by taking thought. It is not possible if we regard love as a law which must be obeyed. Love is indeed the law of life; but it is most surely obeyed when we are not conscious of obedience to any law. It is obeyed when the sorrows of others arouse our sympathies, when their needs prompt us to forget our own needs and meet those of our friends and neighbors. We become most truly ourselves when we forget ourselves; for it is preoccupation with self which prematurely arrests the growth of the self and confines it to too narrow limits. The peace of love is thus the ultimate peace of being or becoming what we truly are: creatures who do not live in and for themselves, but find themselves in the life of the community, and finally in God. Obviously, however, this ultimate peace of love is filled with pain and sorrow. It is aware not only of its own pains but also of those of others. The anxious mother keeping a nightwatch over the bed of a sick child has no peace within the limits of understanding. That kind of peace belongs to those who sleep soundly because they have no responsibility for any ailing creature. Yet there can be in the heart of that mother a peace which passeth understanding. Above, beyond, and yet within her anxieties and apprehensions there can be a peace which is the fruit of her complete devotion to the child and the consequence of her fulfillment of the nature and the responsibilities of motherhood.

The servants of the needy who embody the various ministries of mercy, doctors and visiting nurses, social workers and champions of social justice, pastors and all other ministers of need can not have the peace which Epictetus sought after. They become too deeply involved in the suffering to which they minister. Yet the most sensitive spirits of every age have rightly sought after such vocations and found happiness in them. They have experienced the joys which are "three parts pain"; and have touched the fringes of the mystery of the peace of God.

V

It is, however, idle to assume that human society could ever be completely knit together by the perfection of love in which each carries the burdens of all, and the anxieties of each are quieted by the solicitude of all. That is the vision of the Kingdom of God, of the Kingdom of perfect love, which hovers as a possibility and yet impossibility over all human life. Actually the perfect accord between life and life is constantly spoiled by the inordinate concern of each life for its own weal. So pervasive is this self-love that it is sometimes most dangerously expressed when we think we are serving the needs of others; but when really we desire to keep the affairs of others in our power. Human society is full of the friction of cross purposes. The conflict of interest and passion between races, classes, nations, and individuals can be arbitrated into a tolerable harmony by wise statesmanship and astute methods of adjudication and arbitration; but the peace of the world is always, as St. Augustine observed, something of an armistice between opposing factions. There is no perfect social harmony in human history, no peace within the limits of understanding.

The only possible peace within and between human communities is the peace of forgiveness. It is not a peace of perfect accord of life with life, but a peace which is established beyond the frictions of life. And this is a peace beyond understanding. Moralists are always outraged by the idea of forgiveness. They think that it condones evil and is indulgent toward the evil doer. But moralists never fully recognize how much the judgment of the righteous upon the evil doer is below the ultimate and divine judgment. It is the judgment of an unrighteous self upon his fellows. There are of course legitimate judgments of the relatively righteous upon the unrighteous. But even when the unrighteous are as obviously so, as were the recent barbarian rebels against civilization, there is no vantage point in history from which a simple judgment against them can be pronounced. Reconciliation with even the most evil foe requires forgiveness; and forgiveness is possible only to those who have some recognition of common guilt. The pain of contrition is the root of the peace of forgiveness. The forgiveness of God is the readiness of guiltlessness to bear the sin of the guilty. There is an element of this vicariousness in human forgiveness also. Yet a too conscious righteousness never achieves real forgiveness toward an enemy. It is too anxious to censure the evil in the foe; and too oblivious of its own sins. The capacity for forgiveness in man is therefore drawn both from the highest forms of loving righteousness and from the consciousness of common guilt. Forgiveness can not be achieved out of a sense of duty; for it is a form of love which transcends all law and is an offense to the makers and keepers of the law.

Yet it is the only ultimate answer to the complexities of human relations. We will face foes, as well as friends, to the end of history. There are men and nations, groups and classes who prize what we abhor, whose interests run counter to our own, and whose conception of the good contradicts our sense of values. If there were no canons of righteousness by which conflicting ideas and values could be judged, human society would be a sea of relativity, a complete anarchy of values and interests. There are indeed proximate standards of justice and virtue by which society judges the most explicit forms of vice and rebellion against order. But there are no perfectly disinterested judges: all of them are partially involved in the contest of life with life which their judgments seek to arbitrate. They are interested participants in the conflict which they seek to compose. Insofar as they are righteous and just but without mercy, they may repress evil but they can not induce true repentance in the evil doer. Insofar as they are righteous, but unconscious of their own unrighteousness—that is, insofar as they pretend to a divine and impartial justice, when in fact they are men who are engaged in an interested conflict with the enemy—their pretension of virtue is a temptation to cynicism rather than repentance in the foe. One of the tragic aspects of our contemporary situation is the fact that the self-righteousness of victorious nations, who pose as the executors of a divine and ultimate judgment, and who consciously and unconsciously obscure their interests in using punishment as a way of maiming the foe's power of competition with them in the struggle of life, prevents the repentance of the foe.

The peace of forgiveness is thus doubly beyond understanding. The roots of it lie in combination of vicarious love and consciousness of sin, which is beyond the understanding of all righteous, and inevitably self-righteous, men and nations. It is possible only to those who by faith know themselves under a judgment which in its final dimension can make no distinction between the self and the enemy, or between the righteous and the unrighteous man. The power and source of this peace is beyond understanding, but is understood by faith. The effect of it is also beyond understanding, in the sense that it is a peace within strife, reconciliation within friction. Its highest perfection is achieved at precisely the point where no one imagines that there is a possibility within the sinful conditions of history to find a perfect accord of life with life, or to achieve a vantage point of disinterested love from which others, but not the self, could be accused of breaking the peace.

VI

If the peace of God which passeth understanding keeps our hearts it will infuse them not only with the peace of forgiving but with the peace of being forgiven. All efforts to arrive at internal peace by moderating passions and desires, or by developing a rational detachment from passion and desire, are only provisionally efficacious. Man is a creature of infinite desires; and the longing for the impossible is the root of both man's greatness and his misery. In Herman Melville's classic, *Moby Dick,* the instinct for caution, moderation and the prudential virtues is symbolically identified with the land; and the impulse toward the infinite is typified by man's longing for the shoreless expanses of the sea. "In this landlessness," declares Melville, "alone resides the highest truth, shoreless, indefinite as God" and he thinks it is better to "perish in the howling infinite" than "craven crawl to land." But he is also conscious that the yearning for the infinite is the source of the greatest evil as well as of the highest in man. Ahab, the seafaring hero of *Moby Dick,* achieves an integrity and greatness which is beyond the limits of landlocked prudence. But his boundless ambitions also result in a megalomaniac attempt to destroy the mutual dependence between men, and to achieve a solitary and independent glory.

Melville's modern exposition of the Promethean theme was not appreciated in his day because it was addressed to a generation and a culture which had given itself to the illusion that it had confined all the vitalities of human existence within the canons of prudence and common sense. The real situation is that the miseries as well as the glories of man's life are the fruit of his boundlessness. The desire of man to be related to the whole of life, to give himself to the widest and greatest cause, to sacrifice himself for the highest good, to search after and to know the eternity in which God dwells, is the creative force which breaks the little conventionalities and respectable conformities of life. But the same boundlessness also tempts man to bring the whole of life under his own dominion and to make himself the idolatrous center of the whole scheme of things. If it were possible to separate the two desires absolutely, one might have a guarantee of peace. Peace would be the fulfillment of man's infinite purposes: though such a peace would not be too simple, for how are boundless possibilities to be realized?

But actually the human situation is more complicated. The love of God and the love of self are curiously intermingled in life. The worship of God and the worship of self confronts us in a multitude of different compounds. There is a taint of sin in our highest endeavors. How shall we judge the great statesman who gives a nation its victorious courage by articulating its only partly conscious and implicit resources of fortitude; and who mixes the most obvious forms of personal and collective pride and arrogance with this heroic fortitude? If he had been a more timid man, a more cautious soul, he would not have sinned so greatly, but neither would he have wrought so nobly.

The perplexing mixture of good and evil in human history can not be solved by a complacent attitude toward the evil which is mixed with the good. In that case the evil would grow to intolerable proportions. Nor can the evil be eliminated even by the most precise distinctions of the moralists. Every effort to do so creates a form of Christian perfectionism in which the meaningful responsibilities of life are finally disavowed. The kinship between Christian asceticism and oriental forms of life-detachment is significant.

The only possible peace for man, thus involved in the contradictions of existence, is the peace of being forgiven. This is no complacent peace which condones the taint of evil in us. It knows that the evil costs God dearly. But neither is it a peace which prematurely arrests the creative urges of life for the sake of a tranquillity, or which denies the responsibilities of the

THE PEACE OF GOD

self toward others for fear of becoming soiled in fulfilling our duty. It is a peace in which an uneasy conscience is curiously compounded with an easy conscience. This peace rests upon the faith that God is great enough and good enough to resolve the contradiction in which human life stands; and that His mercy is the final resource of His power, by which He overcomes the rebellion of man against his creator.

The moralists always discount this peace because it passes understanding. They want the peace of an easy conscience, which has known and has done its duty. But such a peace always degenerates into a complacent peace, which rests prematurely on its achievements, while some duty remains undone and some responsibility unacknowledged. If on the other hand the boundless and unlimited character of our responsibilities should become apparent to the moralist, and if he should become fully conscious of the taint of self-love which corrupts even our highest moral achievements, he is driven to despair by the disclosure. All forms of simple moralism, whether Christian or pagan, move between the poles of complacency and despair. They pretend to a peace which does not acknowledge the residual chaos in the human soul; or they are overcome by that chaos.

The peace of Christian faith passes understanding because it is God's peace, transferred to us. It is the peace of having and yet not having the perfection of

Christ; of having it only by grace and yet having it the more surely for not pretending that we have it as a right. This peace will offend both rationalists and moralists till the end of history, because it does not conform to the simple canons of either rationality or morality. But it alone does justice to the infinite complexities and contradictions of human existence. Within this peace all of life's creative urges may be expressed and enlarged. There is therefore no simple calm in it. It is as tumultuous as the ocean, and yet as serene as the ocean's depths, which bear the tumults and storms of the surface.

It is the only peace which does not destroy but fulfills all human powers. In that peace we understand that man's life in history is fragmentary and frustrated precisely because it is boundless and unlimited.

www.ingramcontent.com/pod-product-compliance
Lightning Source LLC
Chambersburg PA
CBHW031253230426
43670CB00005B/170